The A-Z of Nostalgia

90's and Early 00's Edition

By Daisy Watson

Copyright © 2020 Daisy Watson

All rights reserved.

Cover design by Daisy Watson

Book design by Daisy Watson

No part of this book can be reproduced in any form or by written, electronic or mechanical, including photocopying, recording, or by any information retrieval system without written permission in writing by the author.

Published by Independent Publishing Network

Printed by Book Printing UK www.bookprintinguk.com
Remus House, Coltsfoot Drive, Peterborough, PE2 9BF

Printed in Great Britain

Although every precaution has been taken in the preparation of this book, the publisher and author assume no responsibility for errors or omissions. Neither is any liability assumed for damages resulting from the use of information contained herein.

ISBNs - 978-1-80049-058-1/978-1-80049-059-8

This book is dedicated to my mum and dad, for providing me with the best childhood a girl could ask for.

And to my husband for putting up with months of crazy 90's throwbacks. Though our life together is often one crazy throwback so perhaps nothing's changed.

INTRODUCTION

Just like Bryan Adams, I had a memorable summer, but it wasn't '69, it was '99. A time spent perfecting "Genie in a Bottle" dance routines and the Tamagotchi giving me my first taste of parenthood. A summer spent religiously sitting by the radio every Sunday, recording the songs from the Top 40 and getting frustrated when the DJ would talk over the last few seconds.

Some might say the 90's, and the early 00's is too recent to class as "nostalgia", yet there were so many aspects of life I wish were still around today. Some of the entries in this encyclopedia are not completely extinct, however I'm sure you'll agree that not everything today is the same as it once was. In this edition we cover all topics from food to toys, music to sports and much more.

Modern life can be difficult for nostalgists like me to get to grips with. There are many questions that arise each day, such as the hidden meanings of emojis. I wouldn't dare ask someone over for moussaka night anymore (yes, that was very awkward!). But it doesn't end there! Only in this day and age could I be discussing moussaka in the privacy of my own home and an advert for a Jamie Oliver moussaka recipe pops up on my social! That is next level creepy. Have we all unintentionally signed up for a version of Big Brother?

Anyway, modern life is very questionable at times, but I can't lie, it's not all bad. I am a fan of the convenience of modern life. If a neighbour asked to borrow some sugar now, I'd say, "you're having a laugh, there's a 24 hour Tesco round the corner". I also appreciate modern technology such as Ipods and how they save a ton of space and money. I no longer must make the life changing decision on what album to take on holiday, I can bring them all!

I'd like to point out I have not compiled this encyclopedia in hopes to go backwards and turn back the clock. This is merely just to spread a smile and bring back a memory. You never know, maybe we could bring back some traditions ready for the generations to come.

So sit back and appreciate some forgotten gems. Let us rediscover some of the things that helped shape you and UK pop culture history.

A1. You know you're a 90's kid when you remember Ben Adams's perfect curtains (the hairstyle) and the tight blue vests of A1. This British-Norwegian band had success with singles "Same Old Brand New You", "Caught in the Middle" and a cover of "Take on Me". Annoyingly pop, annoyingly catchy and annoyingly finding themselves on your Ipod in 2020...

AAH REAL MONSTERS! Nickelodeon cartoon about three monsters, livin' it up in their monster world. A whole generation got to grow up with the weirdest and most random Nickelodeon TV shows. It was dark, there were jokes that would go over kid's heads and all the characters looked like they were dressed for a rock concert.

AALIYAH (1989-2001). R&B singer whose biggest songs were "Try Again" and "More Than a Woman". Aaliyah was effortlessly cool and pulled off the craziest outfits. The white bandana and that Tommy Hilfiger bandeau tracksuit stands out for me. She was so influential. She got signed when she was just 12 years old and then at 15 her success grew, after her album was produced by R.Kelly. Tragically, Aaliyah passed away, along with 8 others in a plane crash on their way back from filming a music video. She was only 22. A tragedy to say the least but her contribution to R&B will not be forgotten.

ABSOLUTELY FABULOUS. British sitcom about two friends who work in the fashion industry. Patsy is one of the most iconic female characters to grace our screens. She was the comeback queen who was never afraid to ugly cry. She showed us that sometimes you just need that shot of vodka to deal with Fleur from Accounts on a Monday morning. Jennifer Saunders created the show and starred as the lead character, Eddy. Jennifer was smashing it during this period with another popular comedy series, "French and Saunders". This was co-created by Dawn French. The pair starred in various comedy sketches and parodies. If you've ever watched any programme about British comedies ever, then you would have seen the "Silence of the Lambs" sketch, hilarious.

ACE OF BASE. Swedish pop group and champions of 90's style. Most popular hits included "All That She Wants", "The Sign" and "Don't Turn Around". They were so big on the Europop scene and Lady Gaga has even said they influenced her a lot in her music.

ACOUSTIC SONGS. The 90's and early 00's churned out a few decent acoustic numbers, which brings me to my first playlist. Some artists may not have been big enough during the era to warrant their own section in this book, so I've come up with a playlist of those one-off acoustic numbers that will hopefully bring back some memories. If not, perhaps you'll discover something you've been missing.

ACOUSTIC AND CHILL PLAYLIST

1. MORE THAN WORDS - EXTREME - 1990
2. HALLELUJAH - JEFF BUCKLEY - 1994
3. STAY - LISA LOEB - 1994
4. ONE OF US - JOAN OSBOURNE - 1995
5. THE PROMISE - TRACY CHAPMAN - 1995
6. DRUGS DONT WORK - THE VERVE - 1997
7. SAVE TONIGHT - EAGLE EYE CHERRY - 1997
8. BABYLON - DAVID GRAY - 1998
9. SITTING DOWN HERE - LENE MARLIN - 1998
10. FOLLOW ME - UNCLE KRACKER - 2000
11. CANNONBALL - DAMIEN RICE - 2002
12. CLOSEST THING TO CRAZY - KATIE MELUA - 2003
13. JCB - NIZLOPI - 2004
14. OTHER SIDE OF THE WORLD - KT TUNSTALL - 2004

ADDAMS FAMILY, THE. They're creepy, they're kooky and they're the ultimate squad goal. The movie was based on the original 60's TV show. In 1991 the pale gang was brought back to our screens. A sequel followed, Addams Family Values, which was just as good. The film stars Anjelica Huston looking like a spicy, gothic goddess and Christina Ricci, as the iconic Wednesday Addams. The film has a colourful array of characters including Cousin It, who should be the face of L'Oreal with those locks. There's also the detached hand that roams around the mansion, The Thing. Oh don't worry, he's armless! Comedy gold, you're welcome.

AEROSMITH. Even though Aerosmith started out in the 70's, the band saw great success in the early 90's. Most successful hits included "Livin on the Edge", "Cryin", "Crazy", "Don't Wanna Miss a Thing" and "Jaded". No doubt, if you were a kid growing up in this era then "Don't Wanna Miss a Thing" was your first awkward slow dance at a school disco. Well I say slow dance, more like a slow shuffle with awkward arms around necks.

AGASSI, ANDRE. Who remembers the luscious locks of 90's tennis favourite, Andre Agassi? I mean he was a great tennis player and everything, but that hair really stole the show. Well it did, until he shaved it all off and then just became another great tennis player. The US sportsman turned pro in the late 80's but won his first Wimbledon in 1992. From there he went on to win 7 singles championships and even an Olympic gold medal. A true tennis ledge!

AGUILERA, CHRISTINA. The early days of Christina were amazing. There were successful hits such as "Genie in a Bottle", which was obviously a tribute to the Disney classic, Aladdin.. right? As well as "What a Girl Wants" and "Come on Over". Boys and girls alike loved her music vids. With us girls perfecting the dance routines. In 2001, she went on to duet with Ricky Martin in "Nobody Wants to be Lonely". Emotional. She was also part of the most killer collab there's been, "Moulin Rouge", with Pink, Mya, Lil Kim and Missy Elliott. Flash forward one year and what on earth happened to our innocent, baby angel Christina, now known as Xtina!? Those dreads, those outfits, the sass! Songs released around this time were "Beautiful", "Dirrrty", "Fighter", "Can't Hold Us Down" and "Voice Within". Don't get me wrong, her music was still bangin' but I couldn't help but long for the days of less eyeshadow and less leather.

AKABUSI, KRISS. Kriss Akabusi dominated the athletics world in the 90's. He won a whole heap of medals at the Olympics, Commonwealth Games and the European and World Championships. His British record for the 400m hurdles still stands today and he went on to gain an MBE in 1992. Once he retired, he became a TV personality, famously hosting the popular show "Record Breakers". His laugh was kind of infectious but just imagine being down a dark alley alone and hearing that laugh behind you.. Kriss is always smiling, motivated and enthusiastic. #BEMOREKRISS.

ALBINO BLACK SHEEP. Website that gained popularity due to the novelty web videos it hosted. Home to classics such as "Ultimate Showdown of Ultimate Destiny", "Urban Legends 3: Ghosts", "Salad Fingers", "Egg Song" and "Llama Song". I'm sorry but "Salad Fingers" was the weirdest, creepiest, thing we ever saw. What even was it!? Surely, TV show "The Mighty Boosh", got major inspiration from this.

ALL THAT. This was must-see TV for 90's teens. Think "Saturday Night Live" for kids. This comedy sketch show on Nickelodeon was the birthplace of many of the Nickelodeon stars we knew and loved. The likes of Amanda Bynes, Kenan Thompson, Kel Mitchell,

Drake Bell, Jamie-Lynn Spears and even Nick Cannon. Dream team!

ALL SAINTS. Girl group who had some great hits that are still enjoyable to this day. Reciting the start of "Never Ever", word for word, with pure attitude! Who did we think we were!? Other All Saints belters included "Black Coffee", "I Know Where It's At", "Pure Shores", "Lady Marmalade" and their version of "Under the Bridge", which actually wasn't too shabby. Sadly, the band suffered a messy break-up. In 2002, the Appleton sisters released a tell-all book, "Together. Some very deep and shocking revelations about the music industry came to light after that, making for a very interesting read.

ALLY MCBEAL. The queen of the skirt-suit and weird hallucinations involving dancing babies. Ally McBeal was a legal comedy-drama series from the US, where all the best fights, dances and conversations happen in the bathroom. If Ally has taught us all anything it's that you can be successful and professional but be a total weirdo at the same time. On that basis, she is my spirit animal.

AMANDA SHOW, THE. This show was actually a spin off of "All That". Very random comedy sketch show for young adults, starring Amanda Bynes and also starring Drake and Josh, who went on to have their own hit Nickelodeon show. Standout sketches included Hillbilly Moment, Crazy "Ma Ha" Courtney, Totally Kyle, The Girls Room/I Like Eggs, Penelope/Amanda Please (which I didn't realise was Amanda in a wig until I was much older. Always slow to cotton on.). Penelope was Amanda's stalker and she created a website dedicated to her, www.nick.com/amandaplease, which used to be an actual site whilst the show was running. You can still access it and any other old websites you fancy looking back on, on "Way Back Machine" https://archive.org/web/ A great website for reminiscing. Anyway, bring in the dancing lobsters.

AMELIE. A whimsical, French fairytale. A gorgeous, Parisian romance movie. Audrey Tatou plays Amelie, a daydreamer who gives her life to helping others find happiness and in doing so, finds her own. Yes, it really is that sickly sweet but it's beautifully put together movie and well acted. You'll also fancy tucking into a creme brulee after watching. Magnifique!

AMERICAN PIE. Series of teen, sex comedy movies from the US. The original was released in 1999, followed by the sequel in 2001 and "American Pie: The Wedding" in 2003. There has been "The Reunion" and various spin offs since then. Everyone must wish their dad was as supportive as Jim's during their teenage years, especially considering the situations Jim found himself in! This movie created the ultimate MILF in Stifler's mum and made sure no one could look at an apple pie or a flute in the same way ever again.

ANASTACIA Pop singer famed for her unique, deeper voice and for wearing different styles of glasses. We all wondered why she wore glasses all the time and it did turn out to be some medical reason. Her biggest hits in the UK were "Outta Love", "Not That Kind", "Left Outside Alone" and "Sick and Tired".

ANASTASIA. Animated children's movie by 20th Century Fox, Disney missed out big time on this classic! Though, Disney did end up buying 20th Century Fox so is it now technically a Disney movie? ANYWAY. The movie follows an orphan named Anya, travelling from Russia to Paris. Everyone keeps telling her that she's a princess, so she goes on this trek to find out if what they're saying is legit. Fun fact, it is loosely based on a true story.

ANDRE, PETER. Australian singer that had us ladies weak at the knees. Posters appeared on many a girl's bedroom wall. The "Mysterious Girl" music vid was the first time 90's kids ever saw a six pack on an actual man and not in the fridge. The 90's were so forgiving in so many ways, I wish cringe music videos were still acceptable now. He had another big hit, "Flava". His other singles released in 1996 included "I Feel You" and "Only One". Looks and pop music aside, Peter Andre seems like a genuinely nice and sweet guy, so you go Peter!

ANGELA ANACONDA. Canadian children's show despised by so many that it had to become a cult classic. The animation was terrifying on so many levels. I still don't know whether they took a human face and put it on a cartoon body or if it was just all animated. Either way it was horrific. To make it worse, the main character's voice was VERY grating. So yeh, you can see why it wasn't welcomed with open arms in the UK.

ANGRY BEAVERS, THE. Animated TV show on Nickelodeon about, yes you guessed it, beavers with anger issues. They were brothers that fought all the time over mundane issues, but when you think about it, if you had their life, you'd be pretty narked too.

ANIMAL ARK. A series of books written by Lucy Daniels, perfect for all the animal lovers out there. They had titles like "Hedgehog in the Hall" and "Badger in the Basement". The book covers were beautifully illustrated. Each book was a different story about an animal, usually in need of rescuing or rehoming. The books were an emotional rollercoaster but often there was a light at the end of the tunnel, so all ended well.

ANIMAL PRINT. Not all Kat Slater, animal print can actually be very tasteful and stylish. We saw a vast amount of it in the 90's, favourites included snakeskin, crocodile skin, leopard print and zebra print. Shania Twain rocks the hell out of that leopard print all in one in the video for "Don't Impress Me Much". We all loved Mel B's leopard print cat ears. Snakeskin boots and snakeskin trousers were a look, but definitely not at the same time. And the mock-croc handbags from the 80's fell into the early 90's as well, so it counts!

ANIMALS OF FARTHING WOOD. All they wanted to do was cross a road, but no one would let them would they!? Emotional whirlwind is an understatement. Whilst the book was written back in 1979 by Colin Dann, BBC's animated TV series, aired in the 90's. It was one of my favourites as a kid and boy was I invested. This show was hardcore, the series was total carnage with brutal animal deaths, and not even caused by humans all the time. These creatures savaged each other for sport!

ANIMANIACS. A children's cartoon about three siblings, jam packed with innuendos and jokes for the adults. The two brothers were clearly womanizers, which made me feel sorry for the sister. The reason I've referred to the Animaniacs as siblings is because I have no idea what they are. Are they dogs? Rabbits? Monkeys? Not a clue.

ANOTHER LEVEL. Boy band who released the raunchiest song ever to hit UK charts, "Freak Me". We were way too embarrassed to sing it in front of mum and dad! Other big songs by this band included "From the Heart", "I Want You For Myself" and "Be Alone No More". One of the members, Dane Bowers, had some solo success. Most notably "Out of Your Mind" with Victoria Beckham and "Buggin" with True Steppers.

ANTZ. Dreamworks movie often confused with "A Bugs Life". Some would argue that "Antz" is the best insect-based movie ever. The movie follows an ant named Z (voiced by no other than Woody Allen!), who meets and ends up crushing on Princess Bala. The ants end up going into battle against termites, things get a little crazy and long story short, Z and the princess end up having to survive in the human world. A solid 7/10.

AQUA. This band is so good because you don't need any musical ability whatsoever to do a great karaoke performance of "Barbie Girl". That's right, this Danish Europop band were the legends that brought us the joy that was "Barbie Girl". I had this single on cassette, I played it endlessly and I have no shame. Other big hits for Aqua were "Doctor Jones", "Cartoon Heroes" and "Turn Back Time".

ARE YOU AFRAID OF THE DARK? Nickelodeon anthology show for young adults, originally broadcast from 1990-1996. It was kid horror, but that doesn't mean there weren't parts that made you pee your pants a little. Think "Tales of the Crypt" but for younger kids. Each episode was a different story. Standouts were the evil clown, the doll, the joker and the lonely ghost. Watch with caution, seriously. I'm still catching up on the sleep I lost because of this show.

ARGOS CATALOGUE. The essential ingredient in the "British Childhood Christmas Starter Pack". The other ingredient being a biro with full ink or a highlighter. Every kid from this era had to allocate a solid half day in November to go through the catalogue with a fine-tooth comb. Sitting at the dining table, frantically circling anything that would make it on the Christmas list and then triple circling around the toy you wanted the most. Your fate was in the hands of the fat man in the red suit and a month of perfect behaviour began.

ART ATTACK. Art show for kids, presented by Neil Buchanan. This show made us feel that with a bit of sticky back plastic and PVA glue we could be the next Picasso. Who remembers those big Art Attacks!? Neil would start gathering random items and laying them out on a field and we would be like, what's going on here? Then, hang on a minute, the camera pans out and it's a tiger made out of socks... MIND BLOWN. Whoever sparked off the rumour that Neil Buchanan could be Banksy, might be onto something there. I'm sure parents couldn't think of anything better to do than clean glitter out of the carpet and pull pipe cleaners out of the sofa.

ARTHUR. A kids show about a loveable aardvark with a catchy, calypso theme tune by Ziggy Marley that never failed to bring a smile. Some truly savage moments in this show, (seriously search "Arthur savage moments" on YouTube). DW was the put down queen! Also, can someone please explain how Arthur wears glasses and headphones nowhere near his ears!? This makes no biological sense whatsoever.

ASHANTI. Sorry Bey and Jay but there was no duo like Ashanti and Ja-Rule. "What's Luv" (which was Fat Joe but had them both featured), "Always on Time" and "Mesmerise" were some of the best hip-hop songs of the era. They also did "Down 4 U", which was so underrated, but was good enough for Whitney Houston to cameo in the music vid so.... Ashanti also did some solo bangers, "Foolish", "Rock Wit U" and "Only U". Ashanti, our days are cold without you.

ASK JEEVES. Refined gentleman, who claimed to be able to answer any question you may have. With a statement that bold Jeeves, you have got to deliver. Sadly, he did not. Ask Jeeves was an internet search engine, with a butler for the LOLs. Ask Jeeves has now become just www.ask.com. Several concerned fans have been questioning the whereabouts of Jeeves. Ask addressed this in their website FAQs and it's all good, Jeeves is just "taking time to relax".

AS TOLD BY GINGER. Totally relatable TV show on Nickelodeon, with the theme tune sang by gravelly voiced goddess, Macy Gray. This is one of those shows you could watch well into adulthood and still enjoy. It follows Ginger, her friends and their struggles through High School.

ATOMIC KITTEN. Three-piece girl band from Liverpool. Original members were Liz, Natasha and Kerry, but Kerry quit 4 weeks after their first single was released so she was replaced by Jenny. We loved their "every other noughties girl" look. They looked like girls you'd see down the town in their new Topshop outfits, Smirnoff Ice in hand. Big hits included "Whole Again", "Right Now" and they did a few covers, "Eternal Flame", "Tide is High", "Be With You" and "Ladies Night".

AUSTIN POWERS. Yeeahhh baby! The Austin Powers movie trilogy, parodying James Bond, was comedy gold as well as being ultra-stylish. The first movie, "International Man of Mystery" with Liz Hurley, introduced us to the Fembots. The second movie "The Spy Who Shagged Me" featured Heather Graham looking particularly spicy and then Foxxy Cleopatra, Beyonce, in the third movie "Goldmember". The music breaks and 60's dancing was a perfect tribute to the era. Mike Myers played multiple roles and had us all wanting our own, naked Mr Bigglesworth. Groovy baby yeh!

B.

B WITCHED. Girl band from Ireland whose debut album was one of the first cassettes I owned. They taught us 90's kids our first bit of French and brought Irish dancing to the masses. Fond memories of me with my blonde pigtails, Irish jigging around my bedroom to "C'est La Vie" and then going all serious, wintery chic for "To You I Belong". Other classics included "Rollercoaster", "Blame it on the Weatherman" and "Rev it Up". Just like many others in the 90's they committed heinous crimes to denim. Double denim will never be a look.

BABE. This movie was a family favourite. A great movie about a talking pig that's putting sheepdogs out of business. Fun fact, the pig was played by 48 different piglets! I guess they didn't want one hoggin' all the limelight... Also, the piglets were given peanut butter to create the illusion of them talking. Greedy pigs! I know, these pig puns are getting boaring….! Regretting the purchase of this book yet?

BABY DOLLS. Important decision when you're about to dabble in the art of parenthood. We had Baby Annabell, Baby Born, Baby Feels So Real (made with gel inside to feel heavy like a real baby), Baby All Gone (the one you force-fed cherries), we even had Baby Wee Wee, very controversial. One of the elderly neighbours down my street used to knit me outfits for my Baby Born. I took this parenting game very seriously. We remember Nickelodeon brainwashing us by showing adverts for these dolls every 15 minutes, conveniently around Christmas time. Forget triple circling in the Argos catalogue, we just ripped the page out and said, "knock yourself out mum".

BABY BUNS. One of THE looks of the 90's, also known as space buns. What female in the 90s didn't rock this hairstyle at some point? In fact, it has come back into fashion and it's still socially acceptable to wear your hair like this. Baby bun royalty includes Gwen Stefani, Mel B, Bjork and of course Princess Leia, the O.G.

BABY G WATCH. There was baby pink and there was baby blue, which one were you? This watch had serious street-cred.

BACKSTREET BOYS. The best boyband of the decade, not counting the angelic harmonies of Boyz II Men. Nick Carter was THE poster boy with his blonde curtains and baggy shirts. This band lived for the token boyband moves, especially the air grab. Top hits that helped you get through the 90's included "Everybody", "Larger Than Life", "Show Me the Meaning", "As

Long As You Love Me", "Shape of My Heart" and "Want It That Way".

BAD GIRLS. Gritty, British soap about the inmates and staff in a female prison. A hard-hitting drama that doesn't shy away from showing viewers the darker side of prison life. If you're staying in G Wing, be prepared for tension, corrupt officers and the two Julies.

BAGUETTE BAGS. Somehow a baguette bag manages to look expensive no matter what you actually spent on it. Very thin in design (hence the name), so if you're taking one out with you then it's a phone, keys and credit card only night. The thin shoulder strap is beautifully feminine. Get one in mock-croc for bonus 90's points.

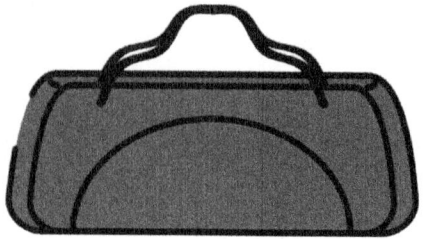

BAKED BEANS PIZZA. Heinz Baked Bean Pizza with Cheese was a thing! I am not kidding here people! It was a taste sensation. There aren't many better combos in this world than beans and cheese. Heinz, what are you playing at? We need this back on our shelves. Thank god it's so easy to make your own!

HOW TO MAKE A CHEESE AND BEAN PIZZA

1. OVEN TO 190 OR GAS MARK 5

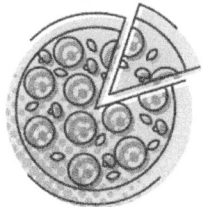

2. CHOOSE YOUR BASE AND SPREAD 3TBSPS OF TOMATO SAUCE ONTO IT

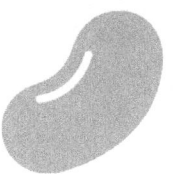

3. INCOMING BEANS! SCOOP THE BEANS OUT OF THE SAUCE, NO ONE LIKES A SOGGY PIZZA. USE ABOUT 75% OF ONE CAN.

4. GRATE 150G MOZZARELLA, SPRINKLE ALL OVER THE PIZZA AND BAKE FOR 15 MINUTES.

BALAMORY. What's the story in Balamory, wouldn't you like to know? Cheery, live-action children's show based in the fictional town of Balamory, Scotland. Almost as cheesy as the cheese and beans pizza mentioned previously.

BALLADS. The ballad game was strong in the 90's with many songs to belt out in your bedroom or shower, but never when there's anyone within ear shot. Below is a playlist of some belters over the era. Also, if you were a little bit scared of the Shakespear's Sister video, you did not suffer alone.

HAIRBRUSH HITS

1. SHOW ME HEAVEN - MARIA MCKEE - 1990
2. EVERYTHING I DO - BRYAN ADAMS - 1991
3. NOVEMBER RAIN - GUNS N ROSES - 1991
4. STAY - SHAKESPEARS SISTER - 1992
5. I WOULD DO ANYTHING FOR LOVE - MEATLOAF - 1993
6. ALWAYS - BON JOVI - 1994
7. I'LL STAND BY YOU - THE PRETENDERS - 1994
8. THE MOST BEAUTIFUL GIRL IN THE WORLD - PRINCE - 1995
9. ALL MY LIFE - K-CI AND JOJO - 1998
10. MY IMMORTAL - EVANESCENCE - 2000
11. HERO - ENRIQUE IGLESIAS - 2001
12. THERE YOU'LL BE - FAITH HILL - 2001
13. WHAT IF - KATE WINSLET - 2001

BALLYKISSANGEL. UK TV show that follows a priest from Manchester who moves to Ballykissangel in Ireland. The Irish countryside is very picturesque, and the show has a slightly quirky edge to it, filled with good humour. Us Brits loved it, it reached 10 million viewers at its peak.

BALTO. Animated movie about a dog/wolf hybrid who was shunned because he looked different to the other huskies. Balto became a hero after battling the elements to get some medicine for some very sick children. The sad reality was Balto just wanted to catch the attention of Jenna, a female husky. Balto knew the way to get to Jenna was to save the child that she so dearly loved from death. The lengths some will go just for a bit of tail! From researching for this book I learnt that this film was based on a true story and is based on a real life Balto from 1925!

BANANAS IN PYJAMAS. One of many children's show of the 90's where the plot made no sense. Why are bananas and teddy bears friends? What do the bananas wear to bed? So many questions, so little time.

BANDANAS. The most badass accessory you could get, bandanas hogged the accessory limelight in the 90's and noughties. Hip Hop acts such as 2Pac and Aaliyah were always sporting a bandana, so naturally we copied them. It wasn't just a headpiece either, ohhh no! You could take the bandana and turn it into a cami/vest top, you could tie it to your trousers, you could even accessorise your bags with them. Versatile!

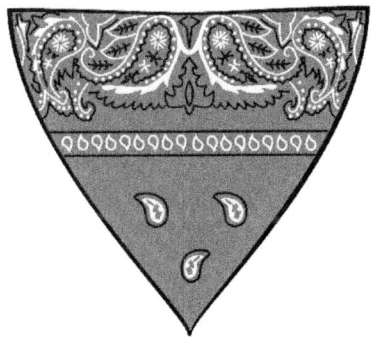

BANG ON THE DOOR. Popular girly brand most famous for "Groovy Chick". This funky gal was on clothing, bedding, lunchboxes, games and much more. Kids that had a purple, Groovy Chick, inflatable armchair in their bedroom were winning at life.

BARBIE GAMES. Barbie Pet Rescue. What a game. This game was you, playing as Barbie, going around saving animals from distress and nursing them back to health. We used to think the graphics were amazing, which is hilarious when you look at today's standards. There were so many other Barbie games that were really good. Titles springing to mind are "Fashion Designer", "Detective Barbie" and "Horse Riding Club". The Barbie website also had some fun games too, especially "Let's Babysit Baby Krissy". I admit I played this on more than one occasion, and I was definitely way too old for it. Who remembers the "Barbie Rockin' Back to Earth Double Bill" VHS movie!? This was on repeat when I was a young kid, good times.

BARNEY & FRIENDS. Young children's show from the USA, jam packed with cheesy songs and dances, convincing kids that learning can be fun. Barney was everyone's favourite purple dinosaur. Though, perhaps mums and dads would disagree after having to sit through the same song at the end of every episode, "I Love You, You Love Me". The best songs from the show included "John Jacob Jingleheimer Schmidt", "Apples and Bananas", "If All the Raindrops" and "B-I-N-G-O".

BARRYMORE, DREW - One of the major actresses associated with the 90's. The beautiful Drew Barrymore starred in some movie classics over the decade - "Scream", "Donnie Darko", "Charlie's Angels","The Wedding Singer", "Never Been Kissed" and "Wayne's World 2". Drew slayed the whole fashion game as well. She had so many looks, from a slip dress to looking effortlessly sexy in men's clothing. Though we may pass on those painfully thin, drawn on eyebrows. Don't worry Drew, we can't get it right all the time, but we love you anyway!

BASEMENT JAXX. English electro duo whose success rose to new heights with hits such as "Red Alert", "Romeo", "Where's Your Head At" and "Do Your Thing".

BAYWATCH. Slo-mo beach runs and red swimwear, don't mind if I do. Main stars of this hit TV show included the likes of David Hasselhoff, Carmen Electra and Pamela Anderson as beach lifeguards. I wonder how many near drownings were genuine. The show started in 1989 but got cancelled after the first series, it survived through syndication. Baywatch went on to become one of the most watched programmes in the world, drawing 1.1 billion viewers a week. There was just something about those lifeguards we couldn't get enough of.

BEANIE BABIES. The toys that everyone collected because we thought they'd pay off our mortgages, but are now in boxes in the attic, waiting for their time to shine again. The nation was obsessed, there was even a Beanie Baby magazine, "Mary Beth's Beanie World". Fancy dress costume idea for your baby, put them in a bear onesie and make them their own TY tag! I know, it's genius. This could also work well for dogs and cats. More popular in the 00's, everyone had one of those rainbow coloured, shiny lizard toys that were filled with sand. Where did they disappear to?

BEAR, THE. Children's book by the incredible Raymond Briggs, released in the 90's. Briggs has been writing and illustrating books since the 70's and is still going strong, with "Ethel and Ernest" being the most recent to get turned into a TV film. An animated short of "The Bear" was aired, but it doesn't get the same hype as "The Snowman" and is sadly rarely shown on TV. "The Man", "Ug" and "Ethel and Ernest" were other books by Raymond Briggs published during this era that are fantastic for adults and children alike.

BEAVIS AND BUTTHEAD. Animated comedy series about two socially awkward, heavy metal loving teenagers. So many of us watched this late at night, whilst consuming a few too many nachos. Benedict Cumberbatch and Neil Patrick Harris need to create a live action re-make. It would be too perfect for words. Beavis and Butthead also had their own movie and a spin off was created called "Daria". Daria was the ultimate moody teenager. The show was way too real at times. Beavis and Butthead in "Virtual Insanity" and "Daria's Inferno" were two very good video games that I would 100% recommend if you were a fan.

BECKHAMS, THE. Victoria and David Beckham, the ultimate power couple. She, a Spice Girl and he, one of the best footballers of all time. We see them together today and they always look sleek and ultra-stylish, Victoria with her fashion house, David with his soccer team and their four perfect kids. But let us just take a minute to remember some questionable looks they had going on in the 90's and 00's. Victoria and David loved coordination. We saw them in head to toe leather, we saw the purple wedding outfits, we saw the white suit and Cinderella dress. Those days where they both had the same length hair and matching black roll necks. I'm sure they would like to forget but we just can't let them.

BEDINGFIELDS, THE. Brother and sister Bedingfield were successful pop acts in their own right. Firstly, Daniel Bedingfield. His two big hits were "Gotta Get Thru This" and "If You're Not the One". Kudos to anyone who can hit that high note. Then his sister, Natasha Bedingfield, who saw one of her hits, "Unwritten" as the theme tune for "The Hills". Her other smash hits were "Single" and "These Words". And then just like that, the Bedingfields vanished from our lives and our charts. Where did they go!?

BEETHOVEN. He slobbered, he drooled and caused nothing but chaos. Funny family movie about a lovable St Bernard who fights against an evil vet, capturing dogs for his evil experiment.

BERNARD'S WATCH. After watching this TV show, we could never look at a watch again without questioning whether we could stop time with it. Why did Bernard never do anything interesting with this power? People used to take the mick and ask him to fetch things for them. Everyone comes crawling when you've got a magic watch.

BETTY SPAGHETTY. This bendy, rubber doll was a much sought-after toy for girls in the early 00's. Think of a mash up between Bratz and Mr Potato Head. Her spaghetti style hair was designed for girls to practise hairstyling. I don't know a French twist from a fishtail braid, so it was clearly wasted on me.

BEYBLADES. Beyblade hype was huge in school playgrounds during the early 00's, mostly with the boys. Crowds would gather at lunchtime to watch kids battle Beyblades, it was highly competitive. The kid that owned the Beyblade stadium was unsurprisingly befriended by all.

BIG BABY POP. Not to be confused with Baby Bop from "Barney". This was a novelty sweet that came in the shape of a baby bottle. You dipped the lolly in the sherbet and sucked it like you were drinking out of an actual baby's bottle. They just slipped away one day and I'm not sure that was a bad thing.

BIG BREAK. Snooker themed game show hosted by Jim Davidson and starring John Virgo. Thanks to a lot of charismatic characters in snooker during the 90's, the sport became exceedingly popular. The show involved contestants answering questions and being paired with a professional snooker player. The first round involved the snooker player potting as many balls as possible. On one of his appearances, Steve Davis only managed to pot one ball, he never lived it down. Jim Davidson was loved by the public and later went on to present another popular game show, "The Generation Game".

BIG BROTHER. Our first insight into reality TV came in 2000 and we couldn't get enough of it. A group of strangers, forced to live together on basic rations, doing demeaning tasks for treats, TV GOLD. We loved it so much that there were two other TV shows, as well as the actual show AND you could watch 24-hour surveillance on E4. We became the TV version of cyber stalkers! Big Brother really was iconic, whether it was the celebrity one or the normal one. It has gone down in TV history and left us with unforgettable moments.

BIG BROTHER'S BIG MOMENTS

1. CRAIG CONFRONTS "NASTY NICK" ABOUT HIS SCHEMING WHEN IT CAME TO VOTING FOR OTHER HOUSEMATES AND IT ENDED UP MAKING YOU FEEL KIND OF SORRY FOR NICK.
2. KINGA GETTING WAY TOO CARRIED AWAY WITH A WINE BOTTLE.
3. MARIO AND LISA DIRTY TALKING IN CODE THROUGH BISCUITS. "I'M DUNKING MY CUSTARD CREME IN MY HOT, MILKY TEA."
4. MAKOSI + ANTHONY + HOT TUB = PREGNANCY SCANDAL
5. "WHO IS SHE!?" THANK YOU NIKKI FOR CREATING BIG BROTHER'S NO.1 CATCHPHRASE.
6. GEORGE GALLOWAY, RULA LENSKA "WOULD YOU LIKE ME TO BE THE CAT?". THE UK WILL NEVER RECOVER FROM THAT.
7. CHANTELLE HAVING TO PRETEND SHE WAS A CELEB AMONGST THE ACTUAL CELEBS AND THEN ENDED UP BAGGIN' HERSELF A CELEB BOYFRIEND! YES CHANTELLE!
8. THE BEST INSULT TO EVER BE DISHED OUT TO A TRIO OF MEN. "TWEEDLE DUM, TWEEDLE DEE, TWEEDLE TWAT" SCIENCE, HOW CAN WE EVER THANK YOU.
9. WHEN GLYNN WAS COOKING AN EGG AND PENNED THIS GENIUS TUNE. "I'M COOKING AN EGG FOR THE VERY FIRST TIME AHMMM". AND WHEN IT GOT REMIXED LIKE THE CILLIT BANG ADVERT.
10. JACKIE STALLONE'S ENTRANCE. THAT IS ALL.

BIG BROVAZ. Big Brovaz were only famous for about a minute and were probably only cool if you were 11 years old, at the time. They're not likely to pop up on anyone's Y2K Spotify playlists, but I think their songs were actually pretty great. Most famous were "Nu Flow", "Favourite Things" and "Baby Boy".

BIG HEADS. Small figures of football players with large heads, standing on a green base. Another similar football figure was "Powerpodz", they came in a chocolate egg, like a Kinder Egg, but with a small footballer inside instead of a toy.

BIG LEBOWSKI, THE. The Dude abides. Cult classic starring Jeff Bridges as "The Dude", in a different take on a detective story. John Goodman and Steve Buscemi also star, to name a few. Fully loaded with bowling appreciation, great wardrobe choices and White Russians (the cocktail, don't get the wrong idea). Two decades later The Dude remains and it looks like he's staying put.

BIG MOUTH BILLY BASS. I had a friend who was obsessed with the "Big Mouth Billy Bass" and by friend, I mean me. A true kitsch favourite! An animatronic fish that sings "Take Me to the River" and "Don't Worry Be Happy", whilst moving its head and tail. Just as good as those singing parrots on a perch from the 80's. Sometimes it's great to let tacky into your life.

BIRDS OF A FEATHER. This show actually started in 1989 but had most of its airtime in the 90's, so it counts. A sitcom centred around two sisters who live together and their man-obsessed neighbour. The show became a comfy staple in British daytime TV.

BJORK. Iconic trend-setter and wonderfully eccentric. Bjork is a pop singer from Iceland. She had a ton of success in the 90's with four albums, "Debut", "Post", "Homogenic" and "Vespertine". Her most widely known song is "It's Oh So Quiet", which is quite frankly, musical bliss.

BLACK BOOKS. British sitcom about a bookshop owner whose customer service levels would be classed as "improvement needed". When his accountant does a runner, he hires a helper to help around the shop. The show takes a surreal turn and is very funny. Dylan Moran is great in the lead role, same goes for Bill Bailey as the helper and Tamsin Greig who runs the shop next door.

BLAIR WITCH PROJECT, THE. Incredibly effective horror movie about three student filmmakers who hear of the legend of the Blair Witch and decide to make a documentary in the woods. What we are watching is their found footage after they disappeared. Very convincing and so well done on a low budget. It may not seem as effective now as it was at the time, but it completely paved the way for other successful point of view horrors such as "Paranormal Activity" and "REC".

BLIGE, MARY J. R&B royalty who first came on the scene in 1992. Since then she has had much success, with hits such as "Everything", "As", "Family Affair", "Dance with Me" and "No More Drama". Blige went from being a backing singer to a household name.

BLINK 182. One of, if not THE best pop punk band ever. Tom Delonge with his unique sound, beautifully suited to Mark Hoppus's deeper tones. Travis Barker looking like a tattooed god on the drums. Pop punk royalty. The album "Take Off Your Pants and Jacket" is all killer, no filler. The album prior, "Enema of the State" had one memorable album cover with great songs including, "Aliens Exist", "What's My Age Again" and "All the Small Things".

BLISS. Popular magazine for young, teenage girls. We had a lot of ups and downs in our early teens. What would we have done without the problem pages making us feel like we're not total weirdos and all alone? "Bliss" answered all our vital questions. "Is it you he wants?", "Are you ready for second base?", "What member of the Sugababes are you most like?".

BLOBBY, MR. If on occasion, you were freaked out by Mr Blobby, it's ok, we all were. Mr Blobby was originally a character on "Noel's House Party" but branched into other guest appearances. He reminds me of one of those stress balls you squeeze, and the eyes pop out. And Americans think they had it bad with Barney, if they saw Mr Blobby they wouldn't sleep for weeks!

BLOCKBUSTER. RIP Blockbuster, we're still not over you. Back in the 90's, watching a film was a family affair and more of an event than it is today. The joy of going to Blockbuster and being allowed to rent videos to watch over the weekend was the best. I did say I like the convenience of modern life, but now it's almost too easy to watch just about anything and it's taken the magic away. When streaming services and subscriptions used to be Blockbuster and that sweet VHS smell.

BLUE. UK boy band, famous for tunes such as "All Rise", "If You Come Back", "Fly By 2", "Too Close" and "One Love". Once they split, Simon Webbe and Lee Ryan had some solo success. Simon gave us "No Worries" and "Lay Your Hands", Lee's included "Army of Lovers" and "When I Think of You". Antony released a solo single "Do You Ever Think of Me". Duncan went down more of an acting path, starring in British soap, "Hollyoaks".

BLUR. Are you Blur or Oasis? The equivalent to today's are you leave or remain question. Blur were the biggest band to come out of the Brit-Pop scene, along with Oasis. They had many successful hits that have not gotten old whatsoever. "Song 2" still gets people jumping up and down on the dance floor. Blur split up in 2003. Lead singer, Damon Albarn, went on to form "Gorillaz" and had a few other musical side projects. Guitarist, Graham Coxon, is still a musician and a visual artist. Alex James, the bassist, swapped park life for farm life and now makes his own cheese. The drummer, Dave Rowntree, became a labour politician. All very different routes you'll agree!

BEST OF BLUR

1. THERE'S NO OTHER WAY - 1991
2. FOR TOMORROW - 1993
3. END OF A CENTURY - 1994
4. GIRLS & BOYS - 1994
5. PARK LIFE - 1994
6. TO THE END - 1994
7. COUNTRY HOUSE - 1995
8. THE UNIVERSAL - 1995
9. CHARMLESS MAN - 1996
10. BEETLEBUM - 1997
11. SONG 2 - 1997
12. COFFEE AND TV - 1999
13. TENDER - 1999

BLUSH PINK. This colour was so popular around the early 00's. Most famously the pink vest top with pink fur attached to it and the the pink velvet cami. Us ladies loved putting cami's and slip dresses over white t-shirts. Can't get much more 00's than that.

BN BISCUITS. BN BN, Doo Doo Da Do Doo, BN BN, Do Do Do Doo. These biscuits came over from France and took the UK's biscuit world by storm. You could opt for a jam centre or a chocolate centre. The biscuits had cheery smiley face on them, automatically making them aimed at kids. Adults like smiles too ya know! The urge for a biscuit pun is strong here, but so far all my jokes have been crummy...

BOB THE BUILDER. Animated children's show with a multi-talented lead character. Meet Bob, not just a builder, but a chart topper. "Can We Fix It" went to No.1 in the UK singles chart in 2000. Not just any No.1 but Christmas No.1! Bob's not doing things by halves! Then he only went and did it again, getting No.1 with his version of "Mambo No.5". We thought he was unstoppable, but his time did come to an end in 2004. A modern reboot has aired in more recent years. Standard.

BODGER AND BADGER. Live action children's show featuring a puppet badger and a quirky human. Badger had an unhealthy obsession with mashed potato. A lot of TV shows back in the day had catchy theme tunes and this one was a jam.

BOP IT. A toy that I would very much like to forget. "Bop It" is a handheld game that tests your reactions. A voice would shout out different instructions, such as "flick it" or "pull it" and you would have to do the action quickly. It was always brought out at parties when you were all sitting in a circle. I used to get in such a fluster with it, so embarrassing. Someone would say "time for a party game" and you were hoping and praying for "Twister", but out comes "Bop It". It's the equivalent of your mum saying, "it's Chinese tonight" and then giving you a Sweet and Sour Pot Noodle.

BORROWERS, THE. Family movie about The Borrowers, who are a family of small people, only 4-inch high in fact! They fight to save their home from a realtor that wants to convert their old house into modern apartments. A charming movie that gives a little insight to how the world is perceived when you're teeny tiny.

BO SELECTA. Adult, comedy sketch show, think X-rated "Spitting Image". Through the use of caricature masks, Leigh Francis mimicked and parodied various celebrities. Pretty offensive and just totally random at times. Best characters included Craig David, Mel B and The Bear.

BOTTOM. Slapstick comedy starring comedy legends, Ade Edmondson and Rik Mayall. They play two flatmates who are unemployed, bored and spend their days scheming and bickering. Slapstick violence at its best.

BOX BRAIDS. Popular hairstyle for women in the 90's. Another popular braid was the hair wrap, often with beads and this would indicate that you had a quality summer holiday.

BOYZ II MEN. R&B vocal group whose harmonies were so satisfying to the ears. If you are unfamiliar, they were the group that did the soundtrack to your most painful college break up. Totally emotional ballads from this band include "End of The Road", "I'll Make Love to You" and "On Bended Knee".

BOYZONE. Before Westlife, there was the original Irish boyband, Boyzone. Boyzone was made up of Ronan Keating, Stephen Gately, Keith Duffy, Shane Lynch and Michael Graham. Top tracks include "Love Me For a Reason", "Picture of You", "All That I Need" and "No Matter What". They also were the kings of the cover version, with their covers actually being pretty good. These included "When the Going Gets Tough", "Words", "Father and Son" and "Baby Can I Hold You". The band split in 1999. Ronan Keating had a very successful solo career. Best songs being "When You Say Nothing at All", "Life is a Rollercoaster", "Lovin Each Day" and "If Tomorrow Never Comes". Other band members went on to dabble in acting and various TV roles. Sadly, Stephen Gately passed away in 2009 due to an undiagnosed health issue.

BRAIN LICKER. Painfully sour, liquid sweet that everyone seemed to buy after school. It looked like a roll-on deodorant and left your teeth with that fuzzy, sugar overload feeling.

BRATZ. A group of 4 fashion dolls including Chloe, Yasmin, Jade and Sasha, popular in the early 00's. Famous for their large heads and pouty lips.

BRAXTON, TONI. Famous R&B songstress who dominated the 90's. Big hits included "Breathe Again", "You're Makin Me High", power ballad "Unbreak My Heart" and "He Wasn't Man Enough". She was beautiful and very fashionable. Most recently Beyonce copied Toni's skinny jean, white vest, leather jacket and cropped hair album cover for a fancy dress do.

BRIDGET JONES'S DIARY. Very popular book and rom-com movie often voted the best rom-com ever made. Painfully British. Renee Zellwegger is fab in the lead role as Bridget, so relatable. Renee also starred in another classic from the era, "Jerry Maguire". Colin Firth and Hugh Grant play the men after her heart, again perfectly cast. They have the most realistic fight scene you'll ever see on screen. I think there's a bit of Bridget in all of us, we all start the year with optimism, we're always on a journey of self-improvement and our parents always call at the most inappropriate times.

BRIT POP. The Brit Pop invasion was a huge part of the music scene in the 90's. You were either team Blur or team Oasis. Whilst these two dominated the scene there were several other fab bands that needed crediting for some of the biggest Brit-Pop hits. Cue playlist.

CLASSIC BRIT POP PLAYLIST

1. CAN YOU DIG IT? - THE MOCK TURTLES - 1990
2. ANIMAL NITRATE - SUEDE - 1993
3. BABIES - PULP - 1993
4. LUCKY YOU - THE LIGHTNING SEEDS - 1994
5. ALRIGHT - SUPERGRASS - 1995
6. COMMON PEOPLE - PULP - 1995
7. GIRL FROM MARS - ASH - 1995
8. WAKE UP, BOO - THE BOO RADLEYS - 1995
9. BEAUTIFUL ONES - SUEDE - 1996
10. CHASING RAINBOWS - SHED SEVEN - 1996
11. SLIGHT RETURN - THE BLUETONES - 1996
12. SUGAR COATED ICEBERG - THE LIGHTNING SEEDS - 1996
13. BITTERSWEET SYMPHONY - THE VERVE - 1997

BROWN LIPSTICK. Brown lipstick worn with a slightly darker brown lip liner for the perfect 90's lip. It graced many a red carpet, along with the over-tweezed eyebrow. No one was afraid to overline their lips back then. J.Lo loved a brown lip, as did Britney Spears, Tyra Banks and many more.

BRUM. The first car you ever loved. Brum drove himself around Birmingham, was pretty intelligent and would get up to no good behind his owners back. This children's show was way ahead of the times with the whole driver-less car thing.

BUBBLEGUM CHARACTERS. Brand of characters including "Nutty Tart" and "Disco Diva". A book, "The Groovy Guide" was released with little bios on each character. They had a website with printable colouring pages. I would often gift them to my mum and dad. These little characters also popped up on greetings cards and posters.

BUCKET HAT. I am THE number one fan of the bucket hat. Made popular in the 90's by hip hop groups, the bucket hat is a great fashion accessory for men and women alike. They come in various materials and colours. A furry baby blue, denim or a Burberry check style is 90's to a tee.

BUFFY THE VAMPIRE SLAYER. Very popular supernatural TV drama, propelling Sarah Michelle Gellar to stardom. A spin off show, Angel, was also a huge success and there were always debates on what show was better.

BUKOWSKI, CHARLES (1920-1994). Incredible German/American poet and writer, whose work was quite often autobiographical. Bukowski is a beat generation authors, with his work quite often centred around sex, drugs, alcohol and living in squalor. Personally I think Bukowski was one of the most thought provoking writers of our time. Here is a taste from one of his novels, "Factotum".

"HOW IN THE HELL COULD A MAN ENJOY BEING AWAKENED AT 6:30AM BY AN ALARM CLOCK, LEAP OUT OF BED, DRESS, FORCE-FEED, S**T, P**S, BRUSH TEETH AND HAIR, AND FIGHT TRAFFIC TO GET TO A PLACE WHERE ESSENTIALLY YOU MADE LOTS OF MONEY FOR SOMEBODY ELSE AND WERE ASKED TO BE GRATEFUL FOR THE OPPORTUNITY OF DOING SO"
- FACTOTUM, CHARLES BUKOWSKI

BUM BAGS. I'm sad to say the bum bag is no longer a distant memory, it has seen a revival. It's back with a vengeance on runways, blogs and in magazines. The bumbag has now gone designer. Gone are the days of your grandad on holiday, shirt tucked in shorts, with a luminous bum bag for carrying the essentials.

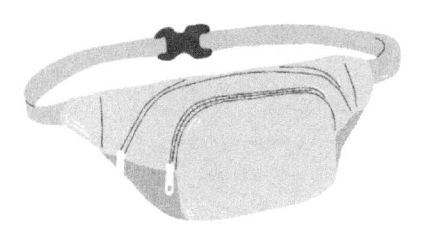

BURTON, TIM. The legendary movie director that is Tim Burton brought us some movie classics in the 90's/early 00's. We saw the birth of a beautiful partnership with him and Johnny Depp working on many movies together. We then saw a second beautiful partnership when he and Helena Bonham-Carter began dating. A gothic power couple to say the least.

BURTON'S FINEST

1. EDWARD SCISSORHANDS - 1990
2. BATMAN RETURNS - 1992
3. THE NIGHTMARE BEFORE CHRISTMAS - 1993
4. ED WOOD - 1994
5. MARS ATTACKS - 1996
6. SLEEPY HOLLOW - 1999
7. PLANET OF THE APES - 2001
8. BIG FISH - 2003

BUSTED. UK pop-rock trio who dominated the charts in the early 00's with hits such as "Year 3000" and "What I Go to School For". The band consisted of Charlie Simpson, Matt Willis and James Bourne. Other noteworthy songs were "You Said No", "Crashed the Wedding" and "Sleeping With the Light on". In more recent years they have been known to tour with another UK boy band, Mcfly, creating the McBusted hybrid. McFly also had success in the 00's with catchy numbers like "Obviously", "It's All About You" and "5 Colours in Her Hair".

BUTTERFLY CLIPS. Every 90's girl went through a phase where she stuck as many of these clips in her hair as physically possible. If you wanted to show off your new heart shaped stick on earrings, then you could use a butterfly clip to clip your hair behind your ear. Clips would often get broken in the process and stepping on them was worse than stepping on Lego.

BUTTERFLY LION, THE. Incredible children's novel by legendary author, Michael Morpurgo. A heart wrenching tale of a young boy who rescues an orphaned, white, lion cub and the unbreakable bond they build. A must read.

BYKER GROVE. Teen drama series that officially came out in 1989 but reached heights in the 90's. If you were young, you felt grown up watching this, it was "cool" and "edgy". Byker Grove was the starting point of Ant and Dec's careers, they played PJ and Duncan. They also released a single under those characters, "Ready to Rumble" and only us Brits could get it to No.9 in the singles chart. I mean we sent a song about living in a blue world to the No.1 spot for goodness sake! Everyone remembers when PJ went blind, even if you did not watch the show, an iconic scene in British TV that we canny forget.

C.

C & A. Clothes shop in the UK that your mum used to drag you to for school uniform. Closed its UK stores in 2000. The shop stocked clothing for all ages and the thought of Woolworths afterwards got you through.

CADBURY'S DREAM. White chocolate bar manufactured by Cadburys. Their answer to Milky Bar. The bar was discontinued in the UK (WHY!) but the lucky citizens of New Zealand, Australia and South Africa still get to enjoy its creamy, chocolatey goodness. Other Cadbury's chocolate bars that have sadly left our shelves are Cadburys Marble, which was white and milk chocolate blended into one, creating a marble effect. Then there was Cadburys Flake - Snow, a flake with a white chocolate inside.

CADBURY'S MONEY BANK. I think I got my entire day's calories from this thing. Red, plastic box where you put 10p in and a Cadburys miniature would come out of it. The novelty lasted a day and then the dispenser was bypassed entirely.

CANDY, JOHN (1950-1994). One of the best loved comedy actors ever and certainly a personal fav. He often played big-hearted buffoons that were so lovable and often his movies would include moments that would pull on anyone's heart strings. Top movies included "Planes, Trains and Automobiles", "Cool Runnings", "Uncle Buck", "Blues Brothers" and "Spaceballs".

CANDYSTAND.COM. Website that hosted candy themed games. I have fond memories of me sitting with my dad playing "Lifesavers Mini Golf", whilst waiting for his online auctions to end. Nostalgia is often triggered by things that remind you of a happier time and this is certainly one of those things.

CAN'T COOK, WON'T COOK. British cooking show presented by British hero, Ainsley Harriott. A celebrity chef would teach someone who cannot cook at all, to cook a dish. Ainsley Harriott was certainly a character, energetic and eccentric to say the least. Very handsy and unintentionally sinister at times.

CAREY, MARIAH. Ultimate diva with the most amazing vocal range. Mariah started out with that signature ringlet hairstyle and emotional ballads. As her career progressed, she moved more into R&B and created one of the most popular festive songs out there. Flawless and fierce, if you got it, flaunt it girl!

THE MARIAH PLAYLIST

1. VISION OF LOVE - 1990
2. EMOTIONS - 1991
3. DREAMLOVER - 1993
4. HERO - 1993
5. WITHOUT YOU - 1994
6. ENDLESS LOVE FT LUTHER VANDROSS - 1994
7. ALL I WANT FOR CHRISTMAS - 1994
8. FANTASY - 1995
9. ONE SWEET DAY FT BOYZ II MEN - 1995
10. ALWAYS BE MY BABY - 1996
11. HONEY - 1997
12. MY ALL - 1998
13. HEARTBREAKER FT JAY-Z - 1999
14. AGAINST ALL ODDS FT WESTLIFE - 2000
15. I KNOW WHAT YOU WANT FT BUSTA RYMES - 2003

CARDIGANS, THE. Swedish pop-rock band that were popular in the late 90's with singles "Lovefool", "Favourite Game", "Erase/Rewind" and "Burning Down the House" with Tom Jones.

CARREY, JIM. Jim Carrey's fame really escalated in the 90's, starring in movies that led him to be the family favourite he is today. Totally unique, zany and maybe slightly mental but you really cannot picture any other actor in any of his lead roles. Below is a list of his amazing movies from the period that are a must see, some may be an acquired taste. If you've already seen them, you should go watch them again, they don't get old!

JIM CARREY FAVOURITES

1. ACE VENTURA - 1994
2. THE MASK - 1994
3. DUMB AND DUMBER - 1994
4. ACE VENTURA: WHEN NATURE CALLS - 1995
5. THE CABLE GUY - 1996
6. LIAR LIAR - 1997
7. THE TRUMAN SHOW - 1998
8. MAN ON THE MOON - 1999
9. ME, MYSELF AND IRENE - 2000
10. THE GRINCH - 2000
11. BRUCE ALMIGHTY - 2003

CARTOON NETWORK. An American TV channel founded in 1992 and owned by Warner Bros. Entertainment. There were so many cartoons that bring back so many good memories. I guarantee just by reading the titles, so many memories will come flooding back to you. As well as creating their own shows, Cartoon Network showed much loved programmes such as "Tom and Jerry", "The Flintstones", "Wacky Races" and much more. The website was filled with amazingly addictive games themed around their shows. Standouts were "Cartoon Summer Resort", "Powerpuff Girls Pillow Fight" and "Scooby Doo's Hollywood Horror".

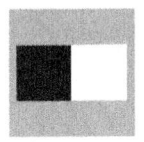

CARTOON NETWORK ORIGINALS

1. DEXTER'S LABORATORY
2. JOHNNY BRAVO - HILARIOUS EVEN FOR ADULTS. AN ELVIS WANNABE WHO THINKS HE'S A STUD BUT IS ACTUALLY A TOTAL FAILURE WITH WOMEN.
3. COW AND CHICKEN
4. POWERPUFFGIRLS - SUGAR, SPICE AND EVERYTHING NICE.
5. ED, EDD AND EDDY
6. COURAGE THE COWARDLY DOG - SOME FREAKY STUFF IN THIS, SERIOUSLY. I RE-WATCHED SOME CLIPS AND CAN'T BELIEVE I WASN'T TRAUMATISED BY THIS SHOW.
7. FOSTER'S HOME FOR IMAGINARY FRIENDS
8. BEN 10
9. THE CRAMP TWINS
10. I AM WEASEL

CASH, JOHNNY (1932-2003). One of the bestselling music artists of all time sadly left us in the early 00's. From his early days of country style rock n roll, to his gospel era and folk sound, Johnny Cash pumped out hit after hit. In his later years he recorded covers of various songs, most famously "Hurt" originally by Nine Inch Nails. Artists lived in fear of Cash covering their songs in case he did it better. He also hosted his own TV show and wrote a captivating autobiography. He fell in love and married fellow country star June Carter. It was widely known how much he adored her. Upon being asked what his definition of paradise was, Cash replied, "this morning, with her, having coffee."

CASPER. Fab children's movie about a friendly ghost, also the best movie to watch at Halloween if you are too chicken to watch an actual horror. Another great performance by 90's royalty, Christina Ricci.

CATATONIA. Welsh pop-rock band fronted by Cerys Matthews, who is classed these days as a "vintage crush". Biggest hits were "Mulder and Scully", "Road Rage" and "Dead from the Waist Down". Cerys also did a duet with Tom Jones of the winter classic "Baby, It's Cold Outside". A song we dub as a winter warmer, yet with very questionable lyrics.

CATDOG. Remember I said a lot of children's shows in the 90's made no sense? CatDog are brothers who happened to be conjoined, one is a dog, and one is a cat. I rest my case.

CATS AND DOGS. A kid's movie about cats and dogs going to war with each other, without the adults cottoning on. My moneys on the dogs, seeing as they're facing a bunch of pussies.

CD:UK/SMTV. Entertainment programmes hosted by Ant and Dec, along with Cat Deeley. We looked forward to Saturday lunchtimes, getting ready for the latest instalment of "Chums" (their parody of friends) and "Wonkey Donkey". You couldn't help but feel sorry for Dec dealing with the clueless people that used to phone in to play Wonkey Donkey, honestly agonising at times.

CEEFAX. To this day, never figured out how to use Teletext and Ceefax. Kids of today will not know the struggles of waiting for the pages to load the football scores or reading the weather in blocky yellow and blue writing. The only way to best describe it for those that don't know is it was an information service, the equivalent to today's red button on digital TV. The weather would take so long to load that the day was probably over by the time you found out the forecast. And by the time you found out the football scores they had probably started the next season.

CELEBRITY DEATHMATCH. Another MTV classic. Celeb Deathmatch was a clay-mation of celebrities randomly wrestling other celebrities. It was kind of like merging WWE with a comedy roast and "Robot Chicken". As far as clay-mation goes, it was pretty gory. Parental guidance advised due to graphic clay violence!

CHANGING ROOMS. D.I.Y programme presented by Carol Smillie and cheeky, cockney, carpenter "Handy Andy", who helped out with the re-modelling. Popular interior designers that featured on the show were Anna Ryder Richardson, Linda Barker and Lawrence Llewelyn-Bowen. Members of the public would come on the show with a room in their house that they wanted doing up and they would leave it in the hands of the designers. We found it hilarious when it all went wrong, and the homeowners hated their new room. I remember one not so funny moment with Linda Barker. She was re-designing a room to house a large, antique teapot collection. Overnight the shelves collapsed, and the valuable collection was totally smashed. At the time I thought the programme had put this in for dramatic effect, but it was totally for real! Poor Linda, I'm sure she must still have nightmares of giant teapots taking over the world.

CHARACTER BUBBLE BATH. Remember those bubble baths that had a plastic bust of your favourite character as the lid. "Teenage Mutant Ninja Turtles", "The Simpsons" and various Disney characters were popular in my household. Bath time also involved a hair wash with L'oreal's "No More Tears" shampoo. The smell screams childhood to me but my eyes were screaming for mercy. No more tears my ass!

CHARMED. Popular US fantasy drama about the Halliwell sisters discovering they're witches after the death of their grandma. They try to live a normal life, but how normal can you get when it turns out you're destined to rid the world of evil.

CHER. We need to talk about Cher and how she introduced the autotune to generations. Cher has been around since the 60's but had a few big hits in the 90's, with "Believe" being one of the biggest anthems of the decade. She also found success with her version of "The Shoop Shoop Song", "Strong Enough" and "The Music's No Good Without You".

CHERISHED TEDDIES. Sweet, little, collectable teddy bear ornaments. Kids born in the 90's probably got one as a Christening gift.

CHICKEN RUN. Stop-motion movie by the makers of "Wallace and Gromit". A parody of "The Great Escape" with chickens imprisoned on a farm instead of humans imprisoned in a prison. The chickens need to get out or else they'll be turned into chicken pies. Hilarity for all the family.

CHOKERS. Accessory that utterly 90's and 00's. There was the choker with a pendant (often a cross or a ying yang), the thick lace strip, the black velvet, the multi strand, the tattoo choker and lastly the studded choker. Gothic chic.

CHRISTIE, LINFORD. Linford Christie had already bagged himself a silver medal in the men's 100m sprint at the Olympics in Seoul. So when the next Olympics came he was 32 and some would say retirement age. But you'd have been wrong to think that about Linford. He only went and won gold in the men's 100m sprint! He is the oldest man to have won the event and still holds the British record. The sprint isn't really the UK's bag and because of this Christie became the third Brit to ever win the event.

CHRISTMAS MOVIES. The 90's and 00's produced some of the best Christmas movies ever and some so bad, we love them. They have been enjoyed worldwide, every year since their release and will continue to delight generations to come.

CHRISTMAS MOVIES

1. HOME ALONE - 1990 - IT STILL PAINS ME WHEN KEVIN'S GETTING READY FOR THE BIG STAND-OFF AND HE MAKES THIS BANGIN' MACARONI CHEESE AND HE JUST LEAVES IT, UNEATEN.
2. FATHER CHRISTMAS - 1991 - RAYMOND BRIGGS BOOK ADAPTATION
3. HOME ALONE 2: LOST IN NEW YORK - 1992
4. MUPPET'S CHRISTMAS CAROL - 1992
5. THE NIGHTMARE BEFORE CHRISTMAS - 1993
6. MIRACLE ON 34TH STREET - 1994
7. THE SANTA CLAUSE - 1994
8. JINGLE ALL THE WAY - 1996
9. JACK FROST - 1998
10. MICKEY'S ONCE UPON A CHRISTMAS - 1999
11. LOVE ACTUALLY - 2003
12. ELF - 2003

CHRISTMAS SONGS. There's nothing like a good Christmas song to set the scene for the most wonderful time of the year. The last few Christmas songs that were any good came out in this period. It's so sad that the Christmas song has been deserted by today's artists. Where has the battle gone for Christmas No.1? Oh well. Get the mulled wine flowin' and the radiator pumpin' (fire cracklin' if you're lucky), and let these festive favourites warm your insides.

A 90'S & EARLY 00'S CHRISTMAS

1. ALL I WANT FOR CHRISTMAS - MARIAH CAREY - 1994
2. PLEASE COME HOME FOR CHRISTMAS - BON JOVI - 1994
3. STAY ANOTHER DAY - EAST 17 - 1994
4. MR HANKEY - SOUTH PARK - 1997
5. BABY IT'S COLD OUTSIDE - TOM JONES FT CERYS MATTHEWS - 1999
6. 8 DAYS OF CHRISTMAS - DESTINY'S CHILD - 1999
7. WHERE ARE YOU CHRISTMAS - FAITH HILL - 2000
8. RUDOLPH THE RED NOSED REINDEER - DESTINYS CHILD - 2001
9. CHRISTMAS TIME - THE DARKNESS - 2003
10. PROPER CRIMBO - BO SELECTA - 2003

CHUCKLE BROTHERS, THE. Barry and Paul Chuckle were a comedy double act, most famous for "Chucklevision", a slapstick, children's TV show. The show summed up what kids shows were like during this time, bonkers. Once the show finished you could find them at many an English seaside resort, along with the likes of Jim Davidson and Cannon and Ball. Gigging, not just sunbathing.

CHUNKY HIGHLIGHTS. From bold blonde highlights to colourful streaks, highlights were a huge trend in the early 00's. Every celeb has had a chunky highlight phase at some point. Most memorably Jennifer Aniston, Kelly Clarkson, Kelly Rowland and Christina Aguilera.

CLEOPATRA. Not the Egyptian queen, but the three-piece girl-band that we had such high hopes for but sadly didn't deliver. Success came with their first hit, "Cleopatra's Theme". The creators of "Despicable Me" must have got major inspiration from the music video. They also released "Life Ain't Easy" and a version of "I Want You Back".

CLUELESS. No.1 teen movim that helped pave the way for movies such as "Mean Girls". Those plaid skirt suits have gone down in movie fashion history. We all wanted Cher's electronic wardrobe organiser. Whatever forever.

COBAIN, KURT (1967-1994). The music world was shook when the tragic passing of Kurt Cobain was announced. Frontman of leading grunge band, Nirvana, he had a natural talent for song writing and performing. So many great songs penned by Cobain, including "In Bloom", "Heart Shaped Box", "Smells Like Teen Spirit", "Lithium" and "Come as You Are". One of the biggest tragedies of the decade.

COLDPLAY. The early 00's saw the birth of what would become one of the biggest bands on the planet. Coldplay came onto the scene in 2000 with their debut album, "Parachutes" and then followed it up with the even more successful "Rush of Blood to the Head". Best singles included "Yellow", "Trouble" and "Clocks".

COLOURED EYESHADOW. Why were all of us females obsessed with that blue frosted eyeshadow look? If it wasn't blue, then it was something opalescent. A shiny, nude pink style eyeshadow was popular as well, though this still works today. I think we'll pass on the blue thanks.

CON AIR. Weird action movie who main stars include Nicholas Cage, John Malkovich, Steve Buscemi and John Cusack. A group of extremely dangerous prisoners are being transferred to a different location via air. They end up hijacking the plane and all hell breaks loose. It's become a cult classic and is worth a watch.

CORRS, THE. Jaunty, Irish pop band, combining traditional Irish sound with pop, country rock. Lovely to hear whilst driving on a sunny day. Check out "Runaway", "What Can I Do" and "Breathless". Their cover of the Fleetwood Mac classic, "Dreams" is actually a pretty solid effort too.

CORSET BAG. Big in the early 00's. It was a small handbag with a thin strap, designed to look like a corset. Some with padding in the bust area and some without. Some were more toned down and stylish, being in all brown suede. Others were tacky and garish in pink and black or PVC style black and red. Me being late to the fashion party, I had the PVC one.

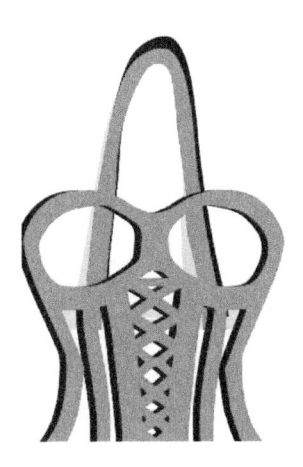

COUSIN SKEETER. A young family invites their cousin to stay with them, only problem is their cousin is a puppet. Skeeter gets himself into all kinds of bad. The situations are unlikely, and the comedy is mostly slapstick. People need to bear in mind the show was designed to entertain kids and if the family never acknowledges the fact that he is a puppet, who cares.

CRACKER. BBC crime drama about a criminal psychologist who has been hired by Manchester police to help them solve serious crimes. Robbie Coltrane was cracking as the miserable psychologist. The show had a fairly dark and dour vibe but there were some bursts of humour. Very atmospheric and pretty classy.

CRASH BANDICOOT. Sadly, no longer considered "cutting edge" graphics, but the Crash Bandicoot video games are still as awesome today. Whilst games like "Pong" are old hat, Crash has really stood the test of time, with the modern remakes just updating the graphics and not much else. The sheer frustration and anguish when you finally got through a level, only to finish with 84/85 boxes. And when "Uka Uka" announces its game over, I think I saw that screen more than the actual game itself!

CRAZY BONES. Popular playground game, like jacks or marbles. Crazy Bones were small plastic figures each with different faces and names. Kind of a weird craze, as they didn't really do anything.

CRAZY TAXI. I reckon a large chunk of cab drivers on the road today are living out their childhood, Crazy Taxi fantasies. The pure adrenaline rush of getting people to their destinations under the time limit. The rage towards those that used to jump out without paying, literally just before their destination.

CRIBS. "This is where the magic happens" said every person on Cribs ever. We loved having a nose around celebrity's cribs but were always a bit sour about the teen cribs. It was a show that was amazing whilst watching it and then when it was over, left you feeling like you failed at life. No one should have to remember that painfully cringe Mariah Carey episode with her countless outfit changes and risqué bathtub antics, but how can we forget?

CRIMPED HAIR. Us 90's chicks crimped our hair and lived to tell the tale.

CROC: LEGEND OF THE GOBBOS. This video game was so good it is crying out for a remake. A similar platform game to "Spyro the Dragon", where Croc must eradicate the bad guy and save those dear, little creatures from getting taken by an evil sorcerer. When you found a Gobbo, Croc would shout "hooray" and it was the cutest thing.

CROFT, LARA. Name a more kick-ass female than Lara Croft. Main character of the "Tomb Raider" games and a total badass. She used to perform flawless backflips and leaps with an elegance desired by so many. The game that showed the world that girls could do it just as good as the guys. Angelina Jolie played Lara in the "Tomb Raider" movie, a perfect casting.

CROW, SHERYL. American, country-pop, singer-songwriter whose biggest hits in the UK were "All I Wanna Do", "If It Makes You Happy", "A Change Would Do You Good" and "My Favourite Mistake".

CRYSTAL MAZE, THE. A popular game show where teams of contestants face multiple challenges in themed rooms. The aim was to collect as many crystals as possible to win the ultimate prize of jumping around in the Crystal Dome. Richard O'Brien presented this show during the 90's and he brought such mysticism to the show. These episodes really give you that warm, nostalgic feeling.

CURTAINS. The male hairstyle, not what curtains your nan had. Curtains are where males grow a long fringe at the front and part it in the middle. I heard a comeback is on the cards. Kings of the curtains included Nick Carter, Leonardo DiCaprio and Johnny Depp.

D.

DA ALI G SHOW. Ali G, played by Sacha Baron-Cohen, is a Jamaican, gangster wannabe from Staines, UK. On his show he interviews real life people on real life subjects, but those getting interviewed don't actually know it's a comedy. Sacha Baron-Cohen also plays other side characters on this show and this is where we first meet Borat and Bruno. His interview with the Beckhams for Comic Relief was definitely a top TV moment of the early 00's. As with most sketch shows not all the sketches are good, but with "Da Ali G Show" lots of them are, so if you're giving it a go for the first time, stick with it.

DANCE ROUTINES. I'm talking "Macarena", I'm talking "Saturday Night", I'm talking "Cha Cha Slide". With the "Cha Cha Slide", I still have no clue what you were meant to do when he said "Charlie Brown". DJ Casper clearly just assumed we should know. All dance routines were taken very seriously, especially at school discos where everyone lined up and if you fluffed it up you looked like a right plum.

DANCE MAT. "Cotton Eyed Joe" was my jam on dance mat, I had the moves down to a tee. I'm surprised my parents don't start rocking backwards and forwards at the sound of a fiddle. We loved the arcade machines and there was always some kid who used to draw a crowd. It was so annoying when you were on a soft mat round a mate's house and it didn't register your move. There were several games for the dance mat, "Dance Dance Revolution" and "Dancing Stage Euromix" were most popular.

DANCING FLOWERPOTS. Kitsch looking flowers that wore sunglasses and start "dancing". Some were activated by sound and some by solar. Popular with windowsills and buskers.

DAPPLEDOWN FARM. A more obscure 90's programme, presented by legend of children's TV, Brian Cant. Brian was helped out by some puppets to put on a show about animals and the farm. Brian was always seen in full tweed get up. The horse would not stop going on about his nosebag, I don't know what Brian was putting in there, but it was clearly something irresistible.

DAVID AND GOLIATH. Popular brand in the 00's. You either owned a t-shirt, a pencil case or a notepad.

DAVID, CRAIG. Garage singer who found fame in the 00's. Biggest hits included "Fill Me In", "7 Days", "Walkin' Away", "Rendezvous" and "Rise and Fall" ft Sting. He also did some awesome tunes with DJ Artful Dodger, "Re-Wind" and "Woman Trouble". Craig David bought garage and the beanie hat to centre stage.

DEMON HEADMASTER, THE. TV series based on books written by Gillian Cross. Had children double taking at their headmasters from 1996-1998.

DEPP, JOHNNY. This actor made his big claim to fame in the 90's with "Edward Scissorhands" and his long lasting, working partnership with Tim Burton. His fresh-faced good looks and textbook 90's style made him a poster boy of the era. He and Winona Ryder gave us couple goals, but it only lasted 3 years, so we changed our minds. Standout movies were "Cry-Baby", "Edward Scissorhands", "What's Eating Gilbert Grape", "Ed Wood", "Fear and Loathing in Las Vegas", "Sleepy Hollow" and "Pirates of the Caribbean: Curse of the Black Pearl".

DESTINY'S CHILD. R&B girl group consisting of Beyonce Knowles, Kelly Rowland and Michelle Williams (though at the beginning it was Beyonce, Kelly, Letoya Luckett and Latavia Roberson.) The girls went on to have successful solo careers too, with Beyonce releasing "Work it Out", "Crazy in Love", "Baby Boy" and "Me, Myself and I" in 2002/2003. Kelly did that amazing duet with Nelly, "Dilemma" in 2002. She later released "Stole" which was so deep, about gun violence and other teenage issues. Michelle focused more on a gospel album and has been very successful in Broadway and acting.

THE BEST OF DESTINYS CHILD
1. BILLS BILLS BILLS - 1999
2. SAY MY NAME - 2000
3. JUMPIN JUMPIN - 2000
4. INDEPENDENT WOMEN P1 - 2000
5. SURVIVOR - 2001
6. BOOTYLICIOUS - 2001
7. EMOTIONS - 2001
8. LOSE MY BREATH - 2004

DIAL-UP INTERNET. Those were the days. All those whirrs and beeps, fingers crossed it would actually connect. Then getting stuck into a chat room or game, having so many lolz and then you hear the dreaded words from your mum, "I NEED TO USE THE PHONE". The internet would be disconnected, and you would sit by your mum whilst she chats away for what feels like an eternity. You would sit there huffing until she would finish and then at the slightest hint of a goodbye you would sprint straight back to the computer. Don't you love the convenience of modern day living? Nonetheless, that dial-up tone brings back so many memories of a childhood well spent.

DIAZ, CAMERON. Coco Chanel once said, "A girl should be two things, classy and fabulous", and that is just what Cameron Diaz is. Her looks in the 90's gave us major outfit envy. She made simple outfits look timeless and chic. Whether it was a turtleneck knit, a flared trouser or a silky dress, she always looked 10/10. The movies she released in the 90's/00's put her on the map as an actor. Check out "The Mask", "My Best Friend's Wedding", "Fear and Loathing in Las Vegas", "There's Something About Mary", "Being John Malkovich", "Charlie's Angels", "Vanilla Sky", "Shrek" and "Gangs of New York".

DIC AND DOM. Children's comedy duo whose TV show, "Dic and Dom in da Bungalow" aired on a Saturday lunchtime. It was a kid's game show and involved lots of gross stuf. If you have ever heard someone shout "Bogies" loudly and then get progressively louder, you have Dic and Dom to thank. Dic's laugh was so contagious and sometimes the kids on the show were uncontrollable and those were always the best bits. It's a shame we don't still live in a world where toilet humour and childish violence are ok for a Saturday lunchtime.

DICAPRIO, LEONARDO. Another huge actor who found fame in the 90's and also found their way onto the walls of many a young girl's boudoir. His first major movie was "What's Eating Gilbert Grape". He was 19 at the time but he looked about 12. He went on to star in one of the biggest movies ever, "Titanic", along with Kate Winslet. They became an iconic duo and have actually remained friends since filming. Other movies to checkout include the modern re-telling of "Romeo and Juliet", "The Beach", "Catch Me If You Can" and "Gangs of New York".

DICKINSON, DAVID. Eccentric antiques show presenter, mostly known for "Bargain Hunt". Doesn't shy away from a fake tan. I would go as far as to say a national treasure. Known for the catchphrases "cheap as chips" and "a right bobby dazzler"

DIDO. Another singer songwriter who vanished off the face of the earth. Her unique vocal style left us with some memorable hits in the early 00's, "Here with Me", "Thank You", "Life For Rent" and "White Flag". She also collabed with Eminem on the huge hit, "Stan".

DIETRICH, MARLENE (1901-1992). German American actress and singer, who starred in movies including "Shanghai Express", "Destry Rides Again" and "Morocco". Her signature pencil thin eyebrows and golden hair made her instantly recognisable. She was so ahead of her time, being very outspoken and throwing gender roles out the window. She was known to wear male clothing yet still ooze feminine sexuality. She had a very sultry singing voice and in her later years, retired from acting and only put on cabaret shows.

DINNERLADIES. British sitcom created by the legendary Victoria Wood. It followed the lives of dinner ladies who worked in the canteen of a factory up North. It was very British in humour and contained a lot of British references, so I'm not sure it would travel well.

DINOSAURS. This show by Jim Henson Productions followed the daily lives of a family of dinosaurs. Baby Sinclair was hilarious, so irritatingly cute, like a child friendly Stewie Griffin. The ending to this show was so traumatic and depressing. I re-watched it recently and it still brought tears to my eyes. You have been warned, the worst ending to a children's show ever.

DION, CELINE. The ballad queen herself! She brought us one of the biggest ballads of all time, for "Titanic", "My Heart Will Go On". Celine began her career in the 80's but she was super successful in the 90's with belters like, "Power of Love", "Think Twice", "Because You Loved Me", "It's All Coming Back to Me Now", "All By Myself" and "That's the Way It Is". She also did a version of "Beauty and the Beast" with Peabo Bryson and it was actually really good. Sorry Angela, forgive me!

DISNEY CHANNEL, THE. TV channel owned by Disney, showing Disney originals and other programmes. Channels that stemmed from this included Disney XD and Playhouse Disney (now Disney Junior). Below is a list of the best shows that graced the Disney Channel during this era. How many did you watch?

BEST SHOWS ON THE DISNEY CHANNEL

1. KIM POSSIBLE - THEME TUNE COURTESY OF CHRISTINA MILIAN
2. LIZZIE MCGUIRE
3. THAT'S SO RAVEN
4. DUCKTALES
5. RECESS
6. TIMON AND PUMBAA
7. GOOF TROOP
8. HOUSE OF MOUSE
9. BEAR IN THE BIG BLUE HOUSE (PLAYHOUSE DISNEY)
10. OUT OF THE BOX (PLAYHOUSE DISNEY)

DISNEY MOVIE RELEASES. Disney and Disney Pixar released so many classic movies during the 90's and early 00's. Some amazing soundtracks to go with them and all vital additions to your movie library.

BEST OF LIVE ACTION

1. THE MIGHTY DUCKS (1992)
2. THE MUPPETS CHRISTMAS CAROL (1992)
3. COOL RUNNINGS (1993)
4. HOCUS POCUS (1993)
5. HOMEWARD BOUND (1993)
6. THE SANTA CLAUSE (1994)
7. 101 DALMATIANS (1996)
8. MUPPET TREASURE ISLAND (1996)
9. GEORGE OF THE JUNGLE (1997)
10. FLUBBER (1997)
11. MIGHTY JOE YOUNG (1998)
12. THE PARENT TRAP (1998)
13. THE PRINCESS DIARIES (2001) - EVERY GIRL READ THE BOOKS BY MEG CABOT AND PRAYED THE SAME WOULD HAPPEN TO THEM.
14. FREAKY FRIDAY (2003)
15. HOLES (2003)
16. PIRATES OF THE CARIBBEAN: CURSE OF THE BLACK PEARL (2003)

BEST OF ANIMATION

1. THE RESCUERS DOWN UNDER (1990)
2. BEAUTY AND THE BEAST (1991)
3. ALADDIN (1992)
4. THE NIGHTMARE BEFORE CHRISTMAS (1993)
5. LION KING (1994)
6. POCAHONTAS (1995)
7. HUNCHBACK OF NOTRE DAME (1996)
8. HERCULES (1997)
9. MULAN (1998)
10. TARZAN (1999)
11. DINOSAUR (2000)
12. EMPEROR'S NEW GROOVE (2000)
13. THE TIGGER MOVIE (2000)
14. LILO AND STITCH (2002)
15. BROTHER BEAR (2003)
16. TOY STORY (1995, PIXAR)
17. A BUG'S LIFE (1998, PIXAR)
18. TOY STORY 2 (1999, PIXAR)
19. MONSTERS INC (2001, PIXAR)
20. FINDING NEMO (2003, PIXAR)

DISNEY SOUND STORIES. Interactive books where the text had pictures in it and the pictures corresponded to a sound on the sound board attached to the book. This was literature's finest work.

DISTRACTION. Hosted by Jimmy Carr, Distraction was a game show where contestants had to answer questions while being distracted in various weird and wonderful ways. For example, there was a round where contestants were naked, apart from wearing these large pants. A snake was put inside the pants and the contestants would then have to answer a series of questions. You can see why having a live snake down there could be very distracting.

DIVA STARZ. Electronic, interactive, fashion dolls with big eyes. There were four to collect, Nikki, Tia, Alexa and Miranda. This time I'd say "Bratz" crossed with "Furby".

DOG SOLDIERS. A cult, werewolf movie that will leave you howling... WITH LAUGHTER. A movie that doesn't take itself too seriously about a group of soldiers fighting off werewolves.

DOGG, SNOOP. AKA Tha Doggfather. Hip-hop artist and rapper who emerged in the early 90's. He became so well known, not just in the rap world but in pop culture as a whole. Snoop has had so many great hits and has featured other great artists in his music. Snoop's best includes "Gin and Juice", "Snoop's Upside Ya Head", "What's My Name", "Beautiful" ft Pharrell and "Drop It Like It's Hot" ft Pharrell.

DOGZ/CATZ. AKA "Petz". Seeing screenshots from this game makes me feel all fuzzy inside. A virtual pet game where you picked a breed of cat or dog and raised it from baby to adult. You could create several and have them become friends and if you're lucky have puppies of your own. There was a "Dogz/Catz" version of the painting "American Gothic" and you could stroke your pets by clicking and moving the mouse. So cute. RIP to all the "Petz" who haven't been fed since 1995.

DOLLY THE SHEEP. Something ground-breaking happened in the 90's. A sheep got cloned and the clone survived and lived an actual life. So unbelievable, it sounds like a Sci-Fi flick. It sparked off a mad ethical debate as they took cells from the original sheep, carried out a procedure called a nuclear transfer and inserted it into another sheep's egg. Dolly was born in the same way any other sheep was born, and she was an exact scientific match to the original sheep. How long will it be until humans can be cloned? Scary thought.

HI, I'M DOLLY

HI, I'M DOLLY

DOLLZ MANIA. Noughties girls! If this hasn't slam dunked you back to the early 00's then I don't know what will. A doll dress-up website where you dressed your "dollz" in various looks and used them as your display pic on MSN. We didn't care that they were pixelated as hell, we took what we were given in 2000! It took us hours choosing the flyest hairstyles and outfits. "Star Doll" was another website that was really good, similar to "Dollz Mania" but had more celebrities that you could dress up.

DOLPHINS. Don't ask me why, but for some reason there was a period of time when we were obsessed with dolphins. Especially dolphin jewellery, ESPECIALLY dolphin earrings.

DONNIE DARKO. 2001 brought us this sci-fi, psychological thriller about time travel and it sort of blew everyone's minds and gave some of us an irrational fear of rabbits. No one had a clue what was going on, yet somehow we still enjoyed it.

DOODLE BEAR. Finally, a toy you could draw all over and destroy and not get yelled at for it! Adorable bear for you to stencil and draw on, then when you wanted to do a different design you just popped it in the wash, and it came out good as new. You could choose from either a pink or blue bear and they had cute buttons for eyes.

DOUG. Another great cartoon from Nickelodeon. It taught us that growing up can get tough and it's ok to fantasize you're a superhero to help get you through it.

DRAGON BALL Z. Popular anime that started in 1989 and went on to have 9 seasons, mostly through the 90's. The show followed Goku and the Z warriors fighting against evil. A second popular anime, "Yu Gi Oh" graced our screens a bit later, in the 00's. "Yu Gi Oh" followed a group of high school students dealing with the trials and tribulations that came with possessing an ancient artifact that had magical powers.

DRAKE AND JOSH. Fresh off of "The Amanda Show", Drake Bell and Josh Peck got their own show. They played stepbrothers who lived together with very different personalities. Another show with a great theme tune which was actually created and performed by Drake Bell himself (he has albums you know!)

DRE, DR. Rapper, producer and so much more. Starting out in hip-hop group, N.W.A, Dr Dre released his first solo album, "The Chronic" in the early 90's. It became one of the best hip-hop albums out there. He also helped bring Eminem and 50 Cent to the top of the charts. He has produced albums and overseen the careers of many other rappers including 2Pac, Snoop Dogg, Xzibit and more. Below is a list of his best rap hits of the era.

TOP DRE

1. DEEP COVER - 1992
2. NUTHIN BUT A G THANG FT SNOOP DOGG - 1992
3. CALIFORNIA LOVE FT 2PAC - 1995
4. FORGOT ABOUT DRE FT EMINEM - 1999
5. GUILTY CONSCIENCE FT EMINEM - 1999
6. STILL D.R.E - 1999
7. WHAT'S THE DIFFERENCE - 1999
8. THE NEXT EPISODE - 2000

DROP THE DEAD DONKEY. British, political comedy about a news company and its workers. The show was great at keeping its material up to date with the current news at the time. Whilst this made the comedy hilarious then, some might find it has since become dated.

E.

EAMON & FRANKEE. We all totally fell for this marketing ploy didn't we!? Hook, line and sinker. Eamon first released "I Don't Want You Back" and then supposed ex-girlfriend Frankee, who the song was about, released her response "F.U.R.B". We thought this was the biggest beef the music industry had seen but Eamon claimed to never have met Frankee and it was a way for her to get a No.1. Well we just don't know what the truth is do we. A similar thing happened with Mario Winans "I Don't Wanna Know" and Noelle's "I Already Know". Trick me once, shame on you, trick me twice, shame on me.

EARTHWORM JIM. Popular platform video game which went on to have several spin offs and a TV show. Navigating the submarine in this game was an art, so much patience was required. The last level was enough to make you quit gaming forever.

EAST 17. Boy band and creators of one of the best Christmas music videos ever "Stay Another Day". Perfectly coordinated and eskimo-looking. The video had a winter vibe but was actually set in space. Best not to question Christmas. Other successful singles, including "Deep", "It's Alright" and "Around the World".

ED THE DUCK. Puppet TV presenter alongside human TV presenters Andy Crane and Andi Peters on CBBC's "In the Broom Cupboard". Ed was tiny, yellow and rocked a green mohawk.

ELLIS-BEXTOR, SOPHIE. Pop singer who stormed on the scene in the early 00's when she lent her voice to "Spiller" by Groovejet. She also had solo success with "Take Me Home", "Murder on the Dancefloor", "Get Over You" and "Won't Change You".

EMINEM. US rapper, Marshall Mathers a.k.a Eminem. If you haven't almost killed your family computer through downloading his songs from Limewire, then have you truly lived? Remember Limewire where there was a 80% chance you'd download a song and it would actually be Clinton talking about sexual relations. Anyway, I digress. Recommendations to listen to include "My Name Is", "Real Slim Shady", "Lose Yourself", "Without Me" and "Stan". Eminem was the king of comedy rap in his early days and through his songs we also got an insight into his family life. There has been a lot of controversy towards Eminem's and his lyrics, but no doubt one of the best rappers of all time.

EN VOGUE. R&B girl group whose harmonies were divine. It's so rare in a band to have every member being lead-singer quality, but En Vogue were just that. Best songs include "Hold On", "My Lovin" "Whatta Man" and "Don't Let Go".

EURO '96. An unforgettable Euros tournament for England, also produced the best football song in the history of football songs, "Three Lions" by Lightning Seeds with David Baddiel and Frank Skinner. They sang "football's coming home" and for a month it felt like it really was. Not only was the tournament held in the UK, we ended up reaching the semi-final! The team were in high spirits and got a bad rap from the press, accusing them of drinking and partying and not training enough. Commentator Barry Davies said, "They had a kind of we'll show you attitude towards the press". Cue Paul Gascoigne, scoring the winning goal against Scotland and doing the famous, "dentist chair" celebration. Of course, it would be Germany to come along and ruin our dreams of getting to the final, but we went down fighting to say the least. It went all the way to penalties and Gareth Southgate officially put our hopes of the trophy to bed. Poor Gareth, he must have felt so bad, and who should come and kick you when you're already down, Pizza Hut!

EURODANCE MUSIC. This style of dance music from our friends across Europe became so popular with some big hits from so many different artists. Love it or hate it, you can't deny it.

EURODANCE MEMORIES

1. EVERYTIME WE TOUCH - CASCADA - GERMANY
2. 2 TIMES - ANN LEE - ITALY
3. HEAVEN - DJ SAMMY - SPAIN
4. LADY - MODJO - FRANCE
5. ONE MORE TIME - DAFT PUNK - FRANCE
6. SPILLER - GROOVEJET - ITALY
7. I NEED A MIRACLE - FRAGMA - GERMANY
8. NOW YOU'RE GONE - BASSHUNTER - SWEDEN
9. CASTLES IN THE SKY - IAN VAN DAHL - BELGIUM
10. DON'T GIVE ME YOUR LIFE - ALEX PARTY - ITALY
11. WHAT IS LOVE - HADDAWAY - GERMANY
12. 9PM (TIL I COME) - ATB - GERMANY
13. SOMETHING - LASGO - BELGIUM
14. BETTER OFF ALONE - DJ JURGEN - THE NETHERLANDS
15. MUSIC SOUNDS BETTER WITH YOU - STARDUST - FRANCE
16. FLAT BEAT - MR OIZO - FRANCE
17. FREE FROM DESIRE - GALA - ITALY/USA
18. MAKE LUV - ROOM 5 - ITALY
19. YOU'RE NOT ALONE - OLIVE - GERMANY
20. YOU DON'T KNOW ME - ARMAND VAN HELDEN - GERMANY/USA
21. I'M A DREAMER - LIVIN JOY - ITALY
22. RHYTHM IS A DANCER - SNAP! - GERMANY
23. FEEL IT - THE TAMPERER FT MAYA - ITALY
24. LOLA'S THEME - THE SHAPESHIFTERS - SWEDEN/UK
25. STARLIGHT - THE SUPERMEN LOVERS - FRANCE
26. SHOW ME LOVE - ROBIN - SWEDEN/USA
27. FLY ON THE WINGS OF LOVE - XTM - SPAIN
28. LOGICAL SONG - SCOOTER - GERMANY
29. CALL ON ME - ERIC PRYDZ - SWEDEN
30. SATISFACTION - BENNY BENASSI - ITALY
31. LOVE DON'T LET ME GO - DAVID GUETTA - FRANCE

EVERYBODY LOVES RAYMOND. US sitcom that's always on TV in the mornings. Everyone has seen at least a snippet of this show. Though they aren't making new episodes anymore, it doesn't feel like it's really ever left us.

F.

FAIRLY ODDPARENTS, THE. A Nickelodeon show about a young boy, Timmy, and his two godparents, Cosmo and Wanda, who happen to be fairies. Featuring cheesy catchy songs by Chip Skylark (voiced by Chris Kirkpatrick from NSYNC). "My Shiny Teeth" would be a great song to play when teaching kids to brush their teeth. Dentists should play it in waiting rooms. "Icky Vicky" was also a jam. There is also a little bit of Mr Crocker in everyone, unsubtle, untactful and sometimes useless at being a human.

FAME ACADEMY. Singing competition that ran for two seasons in the early 00's. I'm sorry but Lemar was the most underrated singer and has definitely not had the career he deserved. You don't hear of any of the contestants anymore. David Sneddon who won the first season has actually gone on to become a very successful song writer, writing songs for the likes of Lana Del Rey, Nicole Scherzinger, Pixie Lott and more.

FARRELLY BROTHERS, THE. These two directed so many great films during the 90's and early 00's. Their movies are always so funny but have heart and meaning behind them as well, making them so memorable. Six movies for your movie collection are "Dumb and Dumber", "Kingpin", "There's Something About Mary", "Me, Myself and Irene", "Shallow Hal" and "Stuck On You".

FAST SHOW, THE. British comedy sketch show. So many quirky and random sketches, standouts include "Jazz Club", "Suits You

Sir" and "Rowley Birkin QC". Paul Whitehouse, Simon Day, John Thompson, Charlie Higson, Caroline Aherne and Arabella Weir were such a strong cast, all with hilarious characters. The show was a favourite of Johnny Depp's and actually starred in one of the "Suits You Sir" sketches.

FATBOY SLIM. Popular DJ from the UK, whose real name is Norman Cook. Not only were his songs killer but he had the most creative music videos. "Praise You" gave birth to the flash mob. "Weapon of Choice" saw Christopher Walken throwing shapes. "Right Here, Right Now" showed us the evolution of the fat man. As well as these bangers there was "Rockafeller Skank" and "Gangsta Trippin". His remix of "Brimful of Asha" by Cornershop, is perfect for a summer's day.

FATHER TED. Very funny sitcom about three Irish priests and their crazy and sometimes unholy adventures. Fecking hilarious! Father Jack was out of control whilst Dougal was idiotic at time. No idea how Ted coped with it all. Oh, you know you want to re-watch it, go on, go on, go on, go on.

FEDERER, ROGER. This tennis legend started his professional career in the late 90's but it was the 2001 Wimbledon where Federer amazed everyone by knocking out the reigning champion, Pete Sampras. It was a shocker because Federer was virtually unknown and ranked 15th in the world at the time. We didn't know it, but we witnessed the start of something special. A record breaker in the making. The Swiss maestro has gone onto great heights, as of June 2020 Federer has won Wimbledon eight times. A true living legend.

FEEDER. One of the most underrated bands on the indie-rock scene. Listen to "High", "Seven Days in the Sun", "Buck Rogers", "Just a Day", "Just the Way I'm Feeling" and "Emily".

FIB FINDER. Popular with young girls, this electronic machine claimed to be able to detect a liar. Your friend would ask you a question and you would press down on a button, give your answer and it would then decide if you were fibbing or not. Sounds legit. The few seconds it took to decide if you were lying were sweat inducing. There was actually a board game element too but who cared, everyone just used it to find out who you were crushin' on at the time.

FIFA. The first ever FIFA to grace our consoles came in December 1993, under the name "FIFA International Football". The game only featured national teams and real names of players were not used. It was revolutionary at the time which is hilarious considering the quality of the FIFA games today. The footballers looked like "Minecraft" characters!

FIGHT CLUB. Often scoring high in the "best movies of all time" countdowns, "Fight Club" was released in 1999 and was like no other. There will be no spoilers in this book so I can't go into much detail. The ending left me with an indescribable, unsettled feeling, not scared but something much deeper. It's hauntingly beautiful, the song chose for the last scene was perfect. You must see it, even if you don't end up loving it, it's just something you have to see. Edward Norton, Helena Bonham-Carter and Brad Pitt give superb performances.

FIREMAN SAM. Originally aired in 1987 but constantly ran throughout the 90's. Kids show that followed Fireman Sam and his fire fighting buddies, saving their small Welsh village from eternal inferno. Makes you wonder how a small village can go through so much turmoil.

FIRST WIVES CLUB. Ok! Ok! I know it's a bit of a guilty pleasure but I j'adore this movie. It's a true girl power movie and the last scene where the main cast burst into "You Don't Own Me" by Lesley Gore is pure cheese fest perfection. Bette Midler and Diane Keaton are brilliant in their roles but my love for Goldie Hawn is just too real. That's it ladies, stick it to the man! Who needs em! Well, at least until you fancy jam on toast and you can't open the jar. Then you quickly realise they have their uses.

FLINTSTONES MOVIE, THE. It's always exciting when your fav cartoon gets turned into a live-action movie. You can't wait to see how close the real actors look to the animation. The "Scooby-Doo Movie" in 2002 was bang on the money, Matthew Lillard as Shaggy and Linda Cardellini as Velma could be the best movie castings in history. Saying that, The Flintstones movie did a good job too. Just slap that wig on John Goodman and you've got Fred Flintstone. Sadly the movie didn't get a great write up from the critics. So what if it's a predictable, family film, sometimes our brains just need a holiday!

FLIPPER. Fun fact, the sounds of the dolphin were not actually from a dolphin, they used kookaburra birds sped up instead. A story of a kid spending the summer with his uncle in Florida and befriending a dolphin. "Free Willy" was another popular movie with similar themes. I don't feel this movie was anything groundbreaking but it was pleasant and as an animal loving kid, it was good enough for me.

FLIP PHONES. There will never be a sleeker phone than the "Motorola Razr", the holy grail of flip phones. That dramatic slam shut when you were done talking to someone is now just a thing of the past. The days when you had to press buttons ten times to write the word "hello". If your flip phone came with a camera, you were next level.

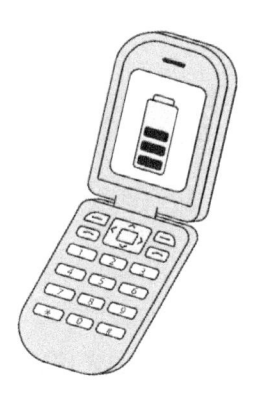

FOLDOVER SOCKS. Thinking back to lower school when every female had white socks that folded over at the ankles with a lace trim. With their name sewn into them, of course.

FOO FIGHTERS. After being the drummer for "Nirvana", Dave Grohl fronted his own rock band. Foo Fighters released their first single in 1995. Dave Grohl said he took the name "Foo Fighters" because he was fascinated by UFOs and that's what they were called in WW2.

ESSENTIAL FOOS

1. BIG ME (1996)
2. MONKEY WRENCH (1997)
3. MY HERO (1997)
4. EVERLONG (1997)
5. BREAKOUT (1999)
6. LEARN TO FLY (1999)
7. ALL MY LIFE (2002)
8. TIMES LIKE THESE (2002)

FOOTBALL. To go into everything that was amazing about football during the 90's and 00's would be a whole other book. Hopefully just the names of these incredible sportsmen will remind you of some of the amazing football moments from years gone by.

TOP GOALKEEPERS
1. PETER SCHMICHAEL
2. DAVID SEAMAN
3. GIANLUIGI BUFFON

TOP DEFENDERS
1. CAFU
2. PAULO MALDINI
3. ROBERTO CARLOS
4. TONY ADAMS

TOP MIDFIELDERS
1. DAVID BECKHAM
2. RYAN GIGGS
3. RIVALDO
4. PAUL SCHOLES
5. DAVID GINOLA
6. ROY KEANE

MORE MIDFIELDERS

1. PATRICK VIERA
2. PAUL GASCOIGNE
3. ROBERTO BAGGIO
4. FRANK LAMPARD
5. STEVEN GERRARD
6. ZINEDINE ZIDANE

TOP ATTACKERS

1. ALAN SHEARER
2. RONALDO
3. RONALDINHO
4. ANDY COLE
5. LES FERDINAND
6. JURGEN KLINSMANN
7. MICHAEL OWEN
8. DWIGHT YORKE
9. TEDDY SHERINGHAM
10. OLE GUNNAR SOLSKJAER
11. IAN WRIGHT
12. ERIC CANTONA
13. DENNIS BERGKAMP
14. THIERRY HENRY
15. GIANFRANCO ZOLA

MEMORABLE MANAGERS

1. ARSENE WENGER
2. ALEX FERGUSON
3. BOBBY ROBSON
4. TERRY VENABLES
5. GLEN HODDLE
6. SVEN GOREN ERIKKSON

FOOTBALL SONGS. Whatever happened to FA cup final songs? Football songs in general seem to be getting less and less. Not saying that's a bad thing, but they did spread joy and got everyone pumped and excited for the game ahead.

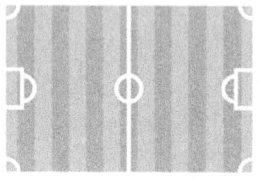

FOOTIE TUNES

1. FOG ON THE TYNE - LINDISFARNE & GAZZA - 1990
2. WORLD IN MOTION - ENGLAND/NEW ORDER - 1990
3. DO THE RIGHT THING - IAN WRIGHT - 1993
4. THREE LIONS - LIGHTNING SEEDS, BADDIEL AND SKINNER - 1996
5. CARNIVAL DE PARIS - DARIO G - 1998
6. VINDALOO - FAT LES - 1998
7. SVEN GOREN ERIKKSON - BELL & SPURLING - 2001
8. BIG BAD LEROY BROWN - VINNIE JONES - 2002
9. WE'RE ON THE BALL - ANT & DEC - 2002

FOOTBALL STICKER ALBUM. The feeling of euphoria when you managed to collect the stickers for an entire team. The page looked perfect They taught us how to barter and negotiate. You felt so deviousness when you managed to trade five stickers for that one sticker you really needed, knowing that those five were really common and you just mugged the other kid right off.

FOOTBALLER'S WIVES. Brace yourself for a major flashback. It was one of THE best programmes of the early 00's. Most of the time it was totally mental. Chardonnay's boobs were set on fire, Amber's dog got accidentally killed, cooked and served as a dish at a party and Jason slept with and got his best friend's mum pregnant. The baby was then born with male and female reproductive organs. WHAT!! There were so many more insane, crazy storylines. I told you it was the best ever.

FORTUNE TELLER. Playground game that required mad origami skills. Your friend would have to choose a number, you would move the fortune teller that number of times. Next, your friend would choose a section and underneath it would reveal their fortune. You would have written things like "will marry Rob and have 4 kids" or "will live in a cardboard box eating cold baked beans". And well, that would be your friend's future cemented.

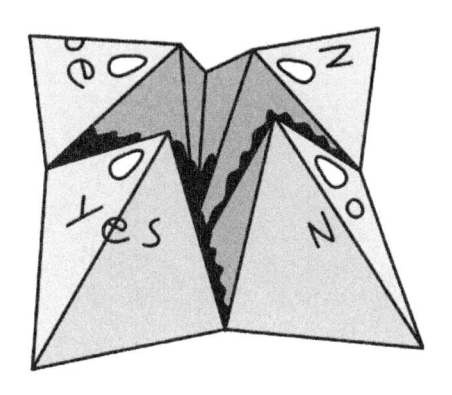

FRANK, PAUL. Fashion designer and artist known mostly for the monkey, Julius. Julius appeared on clothing, accessories, stationery and just about anything you can imagine.

FRASIER. One of America's most loved sitcoms began its 11-season run in 1993. Frasier, himself, is a sarcastic psychiatrist who lives with his father, his father's live-in carer and his father's cute border terrier. Frasier spends a lot of time with his brother Niles. There's a moment when Niles keeps fainting at the sight of blood whilst ironing clothes and sets the apartment on fire. It's rated one of the funniest clips in TV history so give it a watch.

FREE BREAD IN RESTAURANTS. If my bank account could talk it would say "damn this girl can eat". So naturally, I am gutted that this is a dying art. Who didn't love filling themselves up on carbs before a big meal, using the excuse of "it's free so why not!" The bread didn't even have to be top quality, we would settle for slightly sub-par because "it's free so why not!" Bring back bread baskets!

FRESH PRINCE OF BEL AIR. I have never met a 90's kid that doesn't know the words to the Fresh Prince rap. This show propelled Will Smith to Hollywood stardom and boosted the sales of Tom Jones's "It's Not Unusual". The outfits in this show are textbook 90's and fabulous! I loved the contrast between Philly born and bred Will and his bougie Bel-Air family. Why wouldn't you want a sassy butler telling you what's what? Whilst the show was funny, it didn't lack in heartfelt moments. It taught us some life lessons in dealing with disappointment and honesty always being the best policy.

FRIDAY. Hilarious stoner comedy about two friends that get themselves into some deep trouble after taking a dealer's stash. Ice Cube and Chris Tucker are a match made in heaven. In recent years it's gotten more of the praise it deserves. A second and third film were made and there's rumors a fourth could complete the franchise in the future. #BYE FELICIA.

FRIENDS. Pretty much always voted the best US sitcom of all time, "Friends" graced our TV screens for 10 whole years. With it's catchy theme tune courtesy of "The Rembrandts" and six main characters Rachel, Ross, Monica, Chandler, Joey and Phoebe bringing endless laughs. Personally, my fav was Ross, so many hilarious moments with him including the sandwich, the tan, the leather trousers and the sofa. Monica showed us that she and Ross can throw serious moves on the dance floor. Cat owners started serenading their cats with Phoebe's No.1 cat tune, "Smelly Cat". Rachel reminded us that a pink, puffy sleeved bridesmaid dress will never look good on anyone. Joey made us hope for our friends not to show up to our birthday meals, so we can take on all their portions and Chandler taught us that dad jokes are still and will always be cheese. The "Rachel" was a popular hairstyle in the 90's even though Jennifer Aniston herself went on to say she wasn't a fan of the style. The show has such a huge following and there is even a Friends Festival, "Friendsfest", that tours the UK, allowing you to take photographs on replica sets.

FRIENDSHIP BRACELETS. Mostly popular amongst girls. You would either buy or make the bracelet out of coloured strings, beads or scoobie strings and give them to your nearest and dearest.

FROSTED TIPS. How many boys LOVED the frosted tip hairstyle? Often a brown or black hair colour with ice blonde tips. Justin Timberlake was a big fan of the frosted tip, in fact at some stage all of NSYNC rocked a frosted tip. Guy Fieri is still making the frosted tip happen to this day.

FROSTED LIPSTICK. Just like the eyeshadow, us ladies of the 90's loved a frosted lip. Shades of pink, purple and brown were the colours of choice and it's actually a trend that still looks good today. The shine in the lipstick really adds a healthy-looking glow to the face.

FUNFAX. Your life was an unorganised chaos until you put it in your "FunFax". There were also quiz pads and knowledge pads that you could add to your original "FunFax". "Spy File" was a popular add-on.

FUN HOUSE. Pat Sharp and that incredible mullet. This British, children's game show started in 1989 but went on to have 11 seasons, mostly in the 90's. It was wacky, insane and involved gunge. Just what we're looking for from a gameshow! The fun house itself looked like a soft play paradise. Then to make it even better you actually won prizes. And not just small prizes but stuff of dreams, such as a Megadrive or an on-trend watch.

FURBY. Electronic toy that is kind of a cross between an owl and Gizmo from "Gremlins". Some kids loved them, some were terrified by them, I was in the terrified category. Clearly, I wasn't alone, as the look of the modernised version is a lot more friendly. I will never forget begging my parents to get me one for Christmas. They finally did and I thought it would be the start of a beautiful friendship. The reality was, when I opened the Furby and its eyes opened for the first time I was convinced it was the spawn of satan. I remember my mum trying to coax me to play with it, but its eyes were staring into the depths of my soul and I refused to even touch it. My poor parents had to face the fact they had spent a lot of money on something they were going to have to instantly get rid of. My mum has fond memories of her and my dad in hysterics, trying to get the Furby to go to sleep. She recalls the instructions saying to cover the Furby up so it thinks it's dark. My mum and dad put it under a bed duvet and out came a little alien voice, "Oooo i'm scared."

FURTADO, NELLY. Pop singer who climbed the charts with "I'm Like a Bird", a beautiful and uplifting song. Other big songs for Nelly were "Turn Off the Light", "Powerless", "Try" and "On the Radio".

G.

GABRIELLE. British pop/soul singer whose trademark was to have one eye covered, either with a patch, hat or her hair. "Dreams", was a huge along with "Rise" and "Out of Reach".

GAMEBOY. The first ever Gameboy was released in Europe in 1990. Who remembers blowing into the game cartridge when the game wouldn't load? There was no backlight on the Gameboy so if lighting was bad you couldn't see the screen at all, making car journeys at night very difficult. Kids of today won't know the struggles. Sometimes you would get so into the zone that you would forget about the real world. Your mum shouting "it's your brother's turn" brought you back to the sad reality. In 1996 the Gameboy Pocket was released, followed by the Gameboy Colour in 1998 and the Gameboy Advance in 2001.

GAMES, THE. Reality show/competition where celebrities competed against each other in various Olympic style events. Funny and great idea for a reality show, in need of a comeback.

GARAGE MUSIC. One of the best music styles to come out of the UK. Reached heights in the 90's/early 00's and is seeing a modern revival with artists like AJ Tracey. Best described as a blend of R&B and dance, check out the biggest garage hits below.

UK GARAGE PLAYLIST

1. NEVER GONNA LET YOU GO - TINA MOORE - 1995
2. LITTLE BIT OF LUCK - DJ LUCK/MC NEAT - 1999
3. TURN AROUND - PHATS AND SMALL - 1999
4. BODY GROOVE - ARCHITECHS FT NANA - 2000
5. MOVIN TOO FAST - ARTFUL DODGER - 2000
6. RE-WIND - ARTFUL DODGER FT CRAIG DAVID - 2000
7. SORRY - MONSTA BOY - 2000
8. SWEET LIKE CHOCOLATE - SHANKS & BIGFOOT - 2000
9. WOMAN TROUBLE - ARTFUL DODGER FT CRAIG DAVID & ROBBIE CRAIG - 2000
10. DO YOU REALLY LIKE IT? - DJ PIED PIPER - 2001
11. FLOWERS - SWEET FEMALE ATTITUDE - 2001
12. NO GOOD FOR ME - OXIDE AND NEUTRINO - 2001
13. SAMBUCA - DJ LUCK/MC NEAT/WIDEBOYS - 2001
14. 21 SECONDS - SO SOLID CREW - 2001

GEL AND STAMP PENS. The feeling of being a class celebrity when you brought out a brand-new pack of scented gel pens. The joy of knowing your math workbook smelled like grapes. Sending notes in class and stamping the hell out of them with flowers and smileys. Another pen that screams 90's diva is the pink furry pen with a love heart on a spring. Often with a furry diary and pencil case to match.

GET YOUR OWN BACK. Classic game show where children got to take on an adult family member, or anyone they wanted to get revenge on. The adult was often embarrassing to the child in some way. The winning child got to gunge the adult, hence getting their own back. How many of you used to think of taking your mum or dad on there, or even better, your teacher!?

GHOST. One of the most popular romance films ever was released in 1990, starring Patrick Swayze and Demi Moore. Pottery class admissions went through the roof after this one. The movie also sent "Unchained Melody" by The Righteous Brothers back to the top of the charts. A classic for a reason.

GIMME GIMME GIMME. Another weird and wonderful British sitcom about two flatmates. A gay, unemployed actor and his female, unattractive and quirky friend. A bit of a "marmite" comedy as the humour is quite crude and some may find it irritating, but there are some great bits of script and sometimes we need to give trashy humour a go.

GINGHAM. As we have established by now, fashion loves nothing more than to repeat itself. Gingham dresses are one of those pieces that still work today in various colours, though blue and white was the most popular in the 90's.

GIRL TALK. Magazine for young girls that's the equivalent to today's Instagram. My fellow young ladies relied heavily on these magazines for the latest fashion tips, gossip and general life lessons. Before a school disco you would find yourself raiding your stash, finding the pages on "Top Eyeshadow Tips" and "How to Catch Your Crush's Eye". Sadly, your hair and makeup never looked like the cover girl's, but we didn't care.

GLADIATORS. British sports game show hosted by Ulrika Jonsson and John Fashanu (Jeremy Guscott also had a shot at presenting). Members of the public would battle against the athletic adonises that were the Gladiators. Famously, the contestant would go on referee John's first whistle and the gladiator would go on his second whistle. The contestants with the most points would go head to head with each other and face the famous eliminator course with the dreaded travelator!

GLITTER BABES. Once the most sought-after make-up brand. It was available in Boots and it was the introductory makeup for young girls. The nail varnish came in flower shaped bottles and the shiny lip gloss in plastic tubes.

GLOW IN THE DARK STARS. Stick on stars for your bedroom wall that glowed at night, creating an atmospheric ambiance.

GOOD CHARLOTTE. Pop punk band that killed it in the early 00's with "The Anthem", "Girls and Boys" and "Lifestyles of the Rich and Famous". We totally loved Benji's spiky hair and when he had the pink with the leopard sports. So punk.

GOODNESS GRACIOUS ME. Comedy sketch show that pokes harmless fun at British Asian life. Hilarious sketch where they "go out for an English" mocking us Brits going out for an Indian. The cast would go on to form "The Kumars" for their next comedy show, "The Kumars at No.42". Similar comedies, "East is East" and "Bend it Like Beckham", were two very good movies.

GOODNIGHT SWEETHEART. British sitcom starring Nicholas Lyndhurst about a man who is discontent with his life but ends up discovering a time machine. The machine sends him back to the WW2 era where he disguises himself as a MI5 agent. More of a drama with light comedic elements to it.

GOOSEBUMPS. Widely popular series of horror fiction books for children by R.L Stine. The original set consists of 62 books but there has since been various spin off series. A TV series, films and video games have spawned from the original series, with "Slappy the Dummy" as the most well-known character. The book's cover art was amazing. Tim Jacobus needs major credit for his contribution to the success of the Goosebumps series.

GP500 PC GAME. A motorbike racing game released in 1999. In my household, our first ever computer was a "TINY" computer. It came with a selection of free games and this was one of them, along with "Plane Crazy", "Powerboat Racing" and "Creatures". So much enjoyment from these simple games.

GRAF, STEFFI. German superstar tennis player, who was the leading female tennis player of the late 80's and 90's. During her career she won 22 grand slams, over 100 women's titles and even an Olympic gold medal!

GRANT, HUGH. Posh, floppy haired Hugh Grant was king of the rom-com world in the late 90's/early 00's. He is stereotypically British and tends to play himself in most of his movies. He also says "sorry" a lot when it's not needed. A fond favourite of director/writer/producer, Richard Curtis, he starred in "Four Weddings and a Funeral", "Notting Hill", "Bridget Jones Diary" and "Love Actually". Outside of his work with Curtis, he had starring roles in "Pride and Prejudice", "Nine Months", "Mickey Blue Eyes", "Two Weeks' Notice" and "About a Boy".

GREEN DAY. Before their major success with one of the best pop punk albums ever, "American Idiot" in 2004, Green Day had a string of just as awesome hits. There was the emotional "Good Riddance" as well as "Warning", "Waiting", "Minority", "When I Come Around", "Basketcase" and "Hitchin A Ride".

GREY-THOMPSON, TANNI. One of Britain's greatest ever Paralympians. In 1992 she won the London Wheelchair Marathon and then went on to win four gold medals in the Paralympics in Barcelona. Her success didn't end there, with Tanni achieving one gold and three silvers in the next Paralympics in 1996. She retired after the Paralympics in 2004 with 11 golds over her career!

GROUND FORCE. TV show where people's gardens get done up. Presented by the beloved Alan Titchmarsh, alongside Charlie Dimmock and Tommy Walsh. Entertaining for all ages and always nice seeing what they did to the gardens, which always involved some sort of decking and a water feature.

GUNNELL, SALLY. British Olympian, the don of the 400m hurdles. She achieved gold in the 1992 Barcelona Olympics and went onto set a world record in the World Championships in Germany. She is the only female athlete to have had a Commonwealth, European, World Championship and Olympic title at the same time. You go Sally!

H.

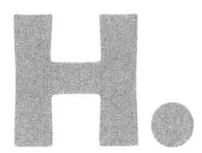

HABBO HOTEL. Social networking website for young adults with themed rooms and personalised avatars. Think Tinder but more cartoon based. Not just a chat room but a site where you could design your own hotel room, play mini games such as "Falling Furni", which was basically musical chairs, and explore the various guest rooms. Relationships were short-lived, the intimacy very forced and the weddings emotional. Famously remembered for replacing any rude words with the word "Bobba", eg, SHUT THE bobba UP! Devious techniques were needed to express your true feelings, like sending out one letter at a time. Whilst in guest rooms you could see other people's chat and some people had no game whatsoever. An avatar with a username of "hackerkid87" asking for your password to give you free coins, come on I fell for that last time, NOT AGAIN. There was also this weird baby cult where some people decided to talk as if they were a baby by putting the letter "w" as the second letter of each word. "Wwheres mwy mwummy?". People were messed up on Habbo.

HAIRY JEREMY. Short lived, stop motion children's TV show from France. It only ran for one season and centred around a caveman and his prehistoric friends.

HANKS, TOM. A true living legend and a modern-day James Stewart. An actor who really is the nice guy of Hollywood. Tom Hanks had a run of amazing movies during the 90's and early 00's. From being rom-com perfection with Meg Ryan to Oscar winning portrayals of real-life heroes, is there nothing he can't do?

90S/EARLY 00S TOM HANKS

1. SLEEPLESS IN SEATTLE - 1993
2. PHILADELPHIA - 1993
3. FORREST GUMP - 1994
4. APOLLO 13 - 1995
5. TOY STORY - 1995
6. SAVING PRIVATE RYAN - 1998
7. YOU'VE GOT MAIL - 1998
8. TOY STORY 2 - 1999
9. THE GREEN MILE - 1999
10. CAST AWAY - 2000
11. ROAD TO PERDITION - 2002
12. CATCH ME IF YOU CAN - 2002

HANSON. Long haired, high pitched singing boy band made up of three brothers who looked the same but were different ages. Their big hit was "MMM Bop", but "Where's the Love" and "I Will Come to You" also did well in the UK chart. Their other success has mostly been in the US.

HARRISON, GEORGE (1943-2001). Beatles lead guitarist and singer-songwriter who sadly left us in 2001. His solo work was very successful, and he also formed a super group with Bob Dylan, Tom Petty, Roy Orbison and Jeff Lynne, "The Traveling Wilburys". His legend and music live on and will continue to do so over many years to come.

HARRY ENFIELD AND CHUMS. First there was "The Harry Enfield TV Programme" and then "Harry Enfield and Chums" followed. They were both comedy sketch shows whose main stars included Harry Enfield, Paul Whitehouse and Kathy Burke.

Popular characters over both shows included the legendary Kevin and Perry, Wayne and Waynetta Slob and DJ's Smashie and Nicey. Just like most sketch shows, not all is hilarious but there is a lot of inspiring comedy in there. There is also a lot of grosse out comedy too which is not so nice.

HARRY POTTER FEVER. How could you have an encyclopedia of the 90's/early 00's and not mention the insanity that was Harry Potter fever. The first book was released in 1997 and the rest is history. The queues outside the book shops were insane. People probably became Harry Potter fans by accident. In true British fashion someone probably saw a queue and just joined it because we are all just so good at queuing and love it so much. Sadly, our letters from Hogwarts must have got lost in the post. The first film came out in 2001. All the candy they order on the train and that huge feast in Hogwarts made us want to lick our TV screens.

HARTMAN, PHIL (1948-1998). Canadian/American actor most famous for being the voice of Troy McClure and Lionel Hutz from The Simpsons. He was a comedian and starred in "SNL" and movies like "Jingle All the Way". His voice was so distinct, and he was perfect at acting smarmy. It's sad to say that a lot of comedians have quite a dark life behind the scenes and the same went for Phil Hartman, tragically passing away in 1998.

HAVAKAZOO. Award winning children's show for preschool age. It was aired on Channel 5's Milkshake slot and was educating children on various subjects. The main character was a robot called Messy who was made from unused objects.

HEELYS. Chunky trainer with a wheel in the heel. Sliding past haters in these bad boys. Every year from the age of 8-12 my New Year's resolution was "Thou shalt master the art of the

Heely". It got to the point where "No shoes with wheels" signs were being put up around the town. Kids would just take out people, recklessly speeding round corners.

HENMAN, TIM. The man behind the hill in London. Tim Henman was Britain's face of hope in the late 90's. Will we get a Wimbledon win? Flash forward to 2002 and Tim Henman has gone out in the semi-final of Wimbledon for the fourth time. Ah Tim, next time, fifth times a charm! Sadly, it was not to be, but the nation seems to embrace failure, so we still chant his name at Wimbledon. Us Brits are so forgiving, out in the semi-finals and he gets his own hill and is still considered a British tennis legend. When China get a silver at the Olympics, they have a breakdown in the corner. I should mention that Henman did win 15 ATP titles during his career, so not all bad.

HENSON, JIM (1936-1990). Legendary puppeteer and animator who created "The Muppets", "Fraggle Rock", "Labyrinth" and so much more. Upon his death Disney released a heart-breaking image of Mickey Mouse consoling Kermit the Frog. The Jim Henson Company had a lot of great shows and films released in the 90's/early 00's including "Dinosaurs" and "Secret Life of Toys". Huge shows such as "Sesame Street", "Muppets" and "Fraggle Rock" were still shown and running during the 90's started a lot further back.

HEPBURN, AUDREY (1929-1993). Actress, humanitarian and fashion icon. Audrey Hepburn was born in Belgium but spent various periods of her childhood in the UK and the Netherlands. She trained as a dancer and got her big break in Broadway in the musical "GiGi". Some of her best movies include "Funny Face", "Sabrina", "Breakfast at Tiffanys", "Roman Holiday" and of course "My Fair Lady". Audrey Hepburn was known for her Bambi like features and famously was dressed by Givenchy. She spent a lot of her later years working as an ambassador for UNICEF. Truly an angelic human being always oozing class, elegance and grace.

HEPBURN, KATHARINE (1907-2003). One of the best actresses of all time, known for her humour, class and distinctive voice. My She was a naturally funny lady, who never took herself too seriously. My top picks include "Bringing Up Baby", "Adam's Rib", "Guess Who's Coming to Dinner" and "The African Queen". She famously dated Howard Hughes but was more known for her love affair with Spencer Tracy, which spanned 9 films and 26 years. You could feel their chemistry and love for one another pour out of the screen.

HEY ARNOLD. Animated show on Nickelodeon, whose main characters included Arnold (football head), Gerald, Helga and Grandpa. A running theme in the show was that Helga always picked on Arnold but she secretly looooved him. This show was cartoon gold that somehow managed to get away with some questionable lines. The revelation that Arnold's skirt thing we thought he wore was actually the bottom of his shirt! How did we not see it!?

HILL, LAURYN. Singer and rapper who had solo success and success with her band "The Fugees". "The Miseducation of Lauryn Hill" was a huge album in the late 90's with big singles being "Doo-Wop" and "Ex-Factor". The Fugees had huge hits with "Killing Me Softly" and "Ready or Not" in 1996.

HOME IMPROVEMENT. Much to parents' annoyance the 90's was full of TV shows that had kids glued to their screens. This sitcom followed Tim Allen, who played a dad who had his own home improvement TV show. Tim Allen brought his whacky comedy style, making him one of the best sitcom dads of the 90's.

HONEYZ. True R&B fans will remember this UK girl group, big in the late 90's. "Finally Found" took a refreshing stance on relationships when other songs were mostly about cussing out your ex boy. "End of the Line" and "Won't Take It Lying Down" were other good songs.

HOUSTON, WHITNEY. The 90's was a killer decade for Whit. The hits she had in the decade were some of her biggest, including "I Will Always Love You", "I'm Every Woman", "I Have Nothing". "When You Believe", "It's Not Right but It's OK" and "My Love Is Your Love". Not just a singer, she also starred as the lead actress in "The Bodyguard" alongside Kevin Costner in 1992. How gorgeous was that jewelled headpiece she wore in that film? She was always flawless, and her curly hair and outfit choices couldn't have been better. Whether it be denim overalls or a slinky black dress, she was always 10/10.

HUBBA BUBBA TAPE. The contests between friends on how much of the tape you could fit in your mouth and chew in one go without locking your jaw. The expectation was buying your Hubba Bubba tape and blowing some mega bubbles. The reality was the bubbles were tiny, popped all over your lips and the flavour would vanish after 10 seconds.

HUGHES, JOHN. Filmmaker responsible for some of the most important questions raised in the 90's. What did Kevin

McAllister's dad do to have a house like that? How can the McAllister's forget Kevin AGAIN? Is Richard Attenborough secretly the real Santa Claus? Top movies released over this period were "Home Alone 1 & 2", "Babys Day Out", "Miracle on 34th Street", "Mallrats", "101 Dalmatians" and "Flubber".

I.

ICE AGE. The first of what would become a very successful franchise was released in 2002. The story of a woolly mammoth, a sloth and a sabre-tooth tiger who find a lost child. They battle the elements and enemies to return the child to its tribe. A super sweet film that shows a cute little kid can melt even the toughest of hearts.

IMAC G3. A walk down memory lane! How big and blocky was the iMac!? The monitors came in a variety of colours. Lots of time was killed on "ClarisWorks" and solitaire? Oh, how the times have changed.

IMBRUGLIA, NATALIE. Natalie Imbruglia blessed us with the absolute tune, "Torn". Fun fact, it is actually a cover! The original song is by a rock band called Ednaswap. Natalie started her career as an actress in "Neighbours" at the beginning of the 90's and then went into singing. This was her main single during the era, but her debut album was very successful.

IMPRESSIONIST SHOWS. This is something we need more of today. Impressionist shows with solid material! "Alistair McGowan's Big Impression" ran from 2000-2003. Alistair McGowan and Ronni Ancona were hilarious as Posh and Becks, Gary Lineker, Ruby Wax and so many more. "Dead Ringers" aired in 2002 whose main star was John Culshaw. He was fab at Ozzy Osbourne and Tony Blair. John also worked on animated adult show "2DTV", which was basically "Spitting Image" but cartoon. Rory Bremner is another fantastic impressionist and had a show "Bremner, Bird and Fortune", these were more political impressions, as Bremner was best known for these during his time with "Spitting Image".

INDIE. The official definition of indie music is "any music that is produced by unsigned or non-major label artists". These absolute tunes from the 90's and 00's certainly became major additions to the UK chart. They have stood the test of time and still get crowds up on their feet. Take a gander at my indie playlist below.

THE INDIE PLAYLIST

1. TWO PRINCES - SPIN DOCTORS - 1991
2. WHAT YOU DO TO ME - TEENAGE FANCLUB - 1991
3. LAID - JAMES - 1993
4. GLORYBOX - PORTISHEAD - 1994
5. LUCKY YOU - LIGHTNING SEEDS - 1995
6. SPARKY'S DREAM - TEENAGE FANCLUB - 1995
7. DESIGN FOR LIFE - MANIC STREET PREACHERS - 1996
8. SPACEMAN - BABYLON ZOO - 1996
9. SUGAR COATED ICEBERG - LIGHTNING SEEDS - 1996
10. THE RIVERBOAT SONG - OCEAN COLOUR SCENE - 1996
11. CLOSING TIME - SEMISONIC - 1998
12. SECRET SMILE - SEMISONIC - 1998
13. DRIFTWOOD - TRAVIS - 1999
14. PUMPIN ON YOUR STEREO - SUPERGRASS - 1999
15. WHY DOES IT ALWAYS RAIN ON ME - TRAVIS - 1999
16. BOHEMIAN LIKE YOU - DANDY WARHOLS - 2000
17. LAST NITE - THE STROKES - 2001
18. JERK IT OUT - THE CAESARS - 2002
19. UP THE BRACKET - THE LIBERTINES - 2002
20. MOLLY'S CHAMBER - KINGS OF LEON - 2003

INFLATABLE CHAIRS. A big fad in the 90's was the uncomfortable, squeaky, inflatable armchair. Often came with cup holders because once you sat in one of those things there was no getting out. If you enjoyed having skin on your thighs, then you wouldn't sit in these during the height of summer. The expectation was so much higher than the reality with this one.

IN MY POCKET. We had puppy, kitten, horse and teddy bear in my pocket. Thanks to my childhood imagination they had so much drama in their lives. Remember that pink and blue wrapper and those cards that had a little bio on each animal? So nostalgic.

INVADER ZIM. Animated, sci-fi kids show that was actually a bit dark. Gir was especially cute and adorable. Human Zim's hair was so current at the time. If you were a young boy in the 90's/00's, no doubt you had some sort of shape shaved into your head.

IRON GIANT, THE. Totally underrated kids' movie that was way heavy. Keep the Kleenex nearby. It's about a young boy becoming friends with an iron giant, who is an alien from another planet. Let's just say the rest of the world doesn't embrace the giant with open arms. Watch it.

ISPY BOOKS. The feeling when you managed to find the items was like the feeling you get when you found the objects in those "Magic Eye" books. People created their own version of "ISpy" books with kids toys and sweets, genius!

ITALIA '90. The year of the John Barnes rap. This world cup may not have been happy memories all round, but it will always be a special one in the eyes of footie fans. England lost to the Germans of all people, on penalties no less, in the semi-final. Of course, we did. The emotion from Gascoigne was heart-wrenching. And the BBC having "Nessun Dorma" as their opening credits was enough to give you chills even before the games even began.

J.

J. LO. The stunning Jennifer Lopez was the Latina goddess of the 90's. She wore that beautiful green plunge dress and that all white outfit with white bandana. How the red carpet has changed! J.LO had some tuuuunes, "If You Had My Love", "Waiting For Tonight", "Love Don't Cost A Thing", "Play", "Jenny From the Block", and "All I Have" ft LL Cool J. J.LO also dabbled in a bit of acting, her biggest roles at the time being "The Wedding Planner" and "Maid in Manhattan".

J17. Teenage magazine, more for older teens so when you were younger you had to hide them so your parents wouldn't discover them. Don't think they would have liked us reading about "The Best Position to Orgasm" when we were just 13! However, the free lip gloss was to die for, so we all looked pretty whilst being scandalous. Another similar magazine was "Sugar".

JACKASS. Movies are still being made even now, but I'm talking about the classic TV series back in 2000. The original Jackass crew were Johnny Knoxville, Bam Margera, Chris Pontius, Dave England, Ryan Dunn, Steve-O, Ehren McGhehey, Jason "Wee Man" Acuña, and Preston Lacy. The show featured the boys getting up to dangerous stunts and pranks, often injuring themselves. Several spin off shows were made including "Viva La Bam" and "Bam's Unholy Reunion" with Bam Margera and "The Wildboyz" with Steve-O and Chris Pontius. A similar show was released in the UK called "Dirty Sanchez".

JACKSON, COLIN. As if life doesn't have enough hurdles as it is, well not for Colin Jackson! Colin Jackson specialised in 110 metre hurdles and still holds the world record for the 60 metre hurdles. He became a much-loved presenter and sports personality as well as smashing indoor and outdoor hurdling events.

JACKSON, MICHAEL. The king of pop continued his reign right through the 90's with an array of pop magic and heartfelt ballads. A year of ups and downs in his personal life but let's just embrace his talent and the music that was loved by so many. Best hits from his 90s period were "Black or White", "Scream" ft Janet Jackson, "You Are Not Alone", "Earth Song", "They Don't Care About Us", "Blood on the Dancefloor" and "You Rock My World".

JAMIROQUAI. UK funk, dance band fronted by Jay Kay, known for his love of hats. Popular songs included "Virtual Insanity", "Canned Heat", "Deeper Underground" and "Little L".

JAMSTER RINGTONES. How much did everyone want a Jamster ringtone back then!? "Crazy Frog", "Sweety Chick" and "Gummy Bear" adverts would always come on whilst you were listening to some music channel, like, "Kerrang" or "Scuzz". They also advertised coloured wallpapers for your mobile, some a bit risqué. We also were well into the polyphonic grooves of chart singles turned into ringtones. Thank god for that mate that actually signed up to Jamster monthly. Oh, and once again, only in the UK could we send "Crazy Frog" to No.1 in the charts.

JAY-Z. US rapper responsible for some totally iconic hits during the 90's/early 00's. "Hard Knock Life", "Izzo", "Bonnie and Clyde" (with future wife Beyonce), "Dirt Off Your Shoulder" and "99 Problems" were all rap anthems.

JAY AND SILENT BOB. The most well-known stoner duo of all time, or at least second to Cheech and Chong. They were originally seen in the movie "Clerks" and the characters were so well loved they got their own movie "Jay and Silent Bob Strike Back" in 2001.

JEEVES AND WOOSTER. This show is what all Americans think us Brits actually are. Sitcom starring British comedy greats, Hugh Laurie and Stephen Fry. Wooster (Laurie) is a well-to-do bachelor who is always getting into sticky situations, leaving his valet Jeeves (Fry) to sort it out. The duo also did "Fry and Laurie" together, which was equally as well loved.

JELLY SHOES. The plastic smell of these shoes transports us right back to the 90's. Sandals for women that always used to cause blisters. Don't get me wrong though, these PVC gems brought so much joy. You could have them sparkly or plain, platformed or flat. So many looks for so many occasions.

JERRY SPRINGER SHOW, THE. Je-rry, Je-rry, Je-rry! American chat show and trash TV at its finest. There is just something about watching other people fail at life that makes you think you aren't doing too badly. A real guilty pleasure. You would flick through the channels, land on Jerry Springer and see a caption like "Dave wants his prosthetic leg back from his girlfriend". It got a hell of a lot weirder than that. There were adults who lived like and were treated like babies, a man that really loved his horse, a woman that married a brick wall or something and so much more. There was speculation that the show was faked due to the craziness of the stories and guests but Jerry Springer himself continues to deny this.

J HORROR. We got scared senseless by those freaky ass Japanese. Total Film magazine rated "Audition" as the scariest film of the 90's. It was noted that so many people walked out of the cinema and some even passed out. In 1998 "The Ring" aka

"Ringu" was released, a lot of you may have seen the US remake but urge you to see the original. We've been scared of TV static ever since. "Hiruko the Goblin" was meant to be a horror comedy, but that film was messed up. "Ju-On: The Grudge", "Tale of Two Sisters", "One Missed Call" and "Dark Water" are all terrifying and again have mostly all been remade by the US. Trust me the subtitles do not ruin it. Thanks to Japan's rich storytelling traditions, the creativity and art of the jump scare really make these movies a horror fan favourite.

JIMMY NEUTRON. Animated TV show created for Nickelodeon about a boy genius and his scientific adventures. Anyone that knows me knows I love a theory, be it conspiracy, supernatural, urban legend or fan theory, I love them all. So, it was to my utmost pleasure that I landed on this fan theory about Jimmy Neutron. Apparently, the theory is that Jimmy and his friends are all genetically engineered, have superpowers and are implanted with a fake family. The rest of the townsfolk are government actors and the town itself is a US government testing ground. RIP childhood.

JOHN, ELTON. Elton John is a music legend and the songs he released during the 90's was awesome. We must thank him for the killer soundtrack to the "The Lion King". Thank you, Elton, for showing me what it's like to feel. Other great hits by Elton during this era include, "Don't Let the Sun go Down on Me" with George Michael, "Something About the Way You Look Tonight", "I Want Love", "Are You Ready for Love (Remix)" and his version of "Candle in the Wind" for Princess Diana.

JOJO. American pop singer whose biggest hits were "Leave" and "Too Little Too Late". "Leave" was about cheating, unfaithful boys and as a 7-year-old I could totally relate.

JUMANJI. Kids movie that could have really been classed as a horror movie. Don't think so? Well how about the fact that an innocent young boy gets sucked into the game for eternity right at the start. Convinced? Kids movies were a lot darker back then.

JUNGLIES, THE. Animated children's show that only ran for 13 episodes and was cruelly cut short. The show followed a group of jungle creatures and their various adventures. Catchy theme tune.

K.

KEEPING UP APPEARANCES. UK sitcom that reminds every one of their nans. Hyacinth Bucket (pronounced Bouquet dears!) was played excellently by Patricia Routledge. Hyacinth is an eccentric snob, who was actually born into a low working-class family but has taken on the deluded persona of a posh lady. Her poor husband Richard puts up with a lot of suffering and her next-door neighbour is terrified of her. A true British classic! Next time the phone rings, answer it with a "The (insert surname) residence, lady of the house speaking."

KELIS. R&B singer who gave us the ultimate angry anthem "Caught Out There". We also loved her single, "Milkshake" and from that album there was also "Trick Me" and "Millionaire ft Andre 3000".

KELLY, GENE (1912-1996). Gene Kelly was an incredible dancer, actor and all-round performer from the US. His most famous role and dance routine would be in "Singin in the Rain". Another famous dance was one he shared with Jerry Mouse from "Tom and Jerry", in "Anchors Aweigh". Along with Fred Astaire, Gene Kelly was the most energetic and skilful male dancer that has graced our screens. His likeable personality, warm smile and pure talent has cemented him in cinema and dance history.

KENAN AND KEL. The golden days of TV really are behind us. Kenan and Kel were one of the best TV duos. Kel with his obsession for orange soda and Kenan shouting "WHY!" all the time. Remember I said that children's TV often poses unanswered questions. Did Kel's parents ever wonder where he was? Also, why did we all believe the actor who played Kel was dead in real life? That's like accidentally eating an apple pip and being convinced you were going to die because your mate said a whole tree was going to grow out of you. Their movie, "Good Burger" was totally separate from the TV show but was still super popular.

KEYS, ALICIA. R&B singer/songwriter who gave us "Fallin", "A Woman's Worth" and "If I Ain't Got You". Alicia is a fantastic pianist and is classically trained. She once played two pianos at the same time on stage. She is super talented.

KING OF QUEENS. Never really too far out of our lives because they constantly show reruns, but King of Queens originally ran from 1998-2007. A US sitcom making Kevin James a household name. James plays Doug, a delivery driver, married to Carrie, played by Leah Remini. He lives a standard working-class life until Carrie's crazy father has to move in with them. The crazy father is played by Jerry Stiller, Ben Stiller's dad and he totally steals the show. Carrie and Doug are a great TV couple. We got so excited when Ray Romano made a guest appearance in an episode. And they say Space Jam was the best crossover!

K'NEX. Construction kits for kids that consisted of interlocking coloured pieces that clicked into place to form various shapes. Some kids who were serious about their construction careers had K'Nex packs with motorised moving parts.

KINSELLA, SOPHIE. Fabulous and funny author who brought us "The Shopaholic" series in 2000. The series began with "Confessions of a Shopaholic" and she went onto release 9 more books. Prior to this, in the mid to late 90s, Sophie Kinsella began her career under her actual name "Madeleine Wickham", but since then she has been writing under Sophie Kinsella. She released 7 books under her actual name, all very good, still in the romantic comedy genre.

L.

LABELLING VHS TAPES. I miss the VHS. smell when you opened the box, the title screens and the fact you could fall asleep during the movie, without being woken up by a loud DVD menu that made you think you'd woken up in the apocalypse. But nothing can take away from the serious organisation skills you learnt when it came to labelling the VHS tapes that you recorded from the TV. Stickers used to come with blank VHS, long and lined so you could keep the writing neat. Then there were the coloured dots if you wanted to organise by colour. I will never forget one amazing family friend of ours. I was the biggest fan of "The Simpsons" but I never got to watch much because it clashed with other things. Anyway, my dad's friend surprised me with a box of VHS. He had been recording every episode of "The Simpsons" that came on for me and I had so many tapes it was incredible. Still to this day one of the best gifts I have ever received.

LAND BEFORE TIME, THE. Actually, released in 1988 but I know for sure that 90's kids adored this movie. A story about a small group of dinosaurs having to fend for themselves and survive to get back to their parents. It's an emotional whirlwind and it will rip your heart out at times. George Lucas and Steven Spielberg were executive producers on the film. Several direct to video sequels were made and a TV series was created after the film's success. There is a scene in the film that I'm still not mentally over and you will know which one it is when you see it.

LAVIGNE, AVRIL. Pop-rock singer from Canada who brought us amazing hits including "Complicated", "Sk8er Boi", "Don't Tell Me" and "I'm With You".

LAWRENCE, MARTIN. After his movie debut in Spike Lee's "Do the Right Thing", Martin Lawrence went on to make some wicked movies. "Boomerang" and "Life" with Eddie Murphy, buddy cop movies "Bad Boys" and "Nothing to Lose". Also, laugh out loud comedies "Blue Streak" and "Big Momma's House". Martin even tried his hand at stand-up and directing during this time. Not only that, during the early to mid-90's he was the lead in his own sitcom, "Martin". Martin was a busy man!

LEAGUE OF GENTLEMEN. Probably one of the weirdest things you'll ever see. A surreal comedy about a village and it's beyond strange residents. It borders on terrifying. We still see Steve Pemberton's character, Tubbs, in our nightmares. Along with Steve Pemberton were co-creators Reece Shearsmith and Mark Gatiss. Definitely a marmite show, but for those who love it, you're not alone, as a movie was made, and a stage show toured.

LEATHER BLAZERS. These blazers still look classy and chic to this day. A leather blazer can look amazing in black, brown or burgundy, paired with a plain top and fitted jeans. Cary Bradshaw would be so proud that this look is still standing the test of time. Step aside biker jackets, you've been centre stage for too long, the blazer is making a comeback.

LEE, BRANDON (1965-1993). Brandon Lee was the son of Kung-Fu legend Bruce Lee and Linda Lee-Cadwell. Brandon was a promising young actor and martial artist himself. He had a few roles in action comedies, but his big breakthrough was going to be as the lead in "The Crow". "The Crow" is a fantastic movie about revenge, stylish and supernatural. It saddens me to say that Brandon Lee didn't make it to the end of filming to see himself in this incredible role. Tragically whilst filming the movie, a prop gun that was meant to fire blanks was faulty and it fired a lead tip that was accidentally lodged in the barrel. The gun was meant to activate fake blood, but the crew sadly realised that Brandon was no longer moving. Tragically shot in the abdomen, he was rushed to hospital but sadly there was nothing the medical staff could do. For the rest of the film Brandon's family gave the studio permission to superimpose his face onto stuntmen. Brandon Lee was buried next to his father in Seattle. A father and son who lived for acting and action who both passed away doing what they loved most.

LEGALLY BLONDE. Starring Reece Witherspoon in her most iconic role, Elle Woods, the pink wearing, chihuahua holding, rich girl who has dreams of being a lawyer, just to win her man back. This movie teaches us to never judge a book by its cover and never underestimate anyone. Elle was one of the most stylish movie characters and it is thanks to her we know about the bend-and-snap.

LEGO RACERS. A Lego, racing game that was available on PC CD-ROM, PS1, Nintendo 64 and Gameboy Colour. Endless fun racing around the Lego Universe. Another great Lego game from this era was "Lego Island 1 and 2", where you played the role of a pizza delivery guy. Trust me, it's better than it sounds.

LIBERTY X. Mixed girl and boy band known for pop songs "Just a Little", "Got to Have Your Love" and "Being Nobody". I remember us girls getting down and dirty at school discos thinking everything about us was "so sexy". We had no clue.

LIGHTHOUSE FAMILY. English duo that were big in the 90's/early 00's. Big hits included "Lifted", "Ocean Drive", "High", "Rain Cloud" and "Lost in Space".

LIL BOW WOW. Child star, rapper and actor from the US. He had a big hit in the UK in 2000 "Bow Wow (That's My Name)" ft Snoop Dogg. He then turned to acting in the family movie, "Like Mike" about an orphan who becomes an NBA star. Another lil man who had success in 2001 was Lil Romeo, with his hit "My Baby".

LITTLE BEAR. Educational, children's animation from Canada. The show follows Little Bear and his animal friends, going on various adventures and learning new things. Great for young children and very underrated. You might think there's not much to this programme but bear with it...

LITTLE BRITAIN. 2003 catchphrase comedy sketch show created by and starring Matt Lucas and David Walliams. This took Britain by storm at the time because it took a whole load of British stereotypes and elevated them to quirky new levels. Most popular characters from the show were Marjorie Dawes,

Andy and Lou and Vicky Pollard. A similar sketch show came out a year later by comedy queen Catherine Tate. "The Catherine Tate Show" was just as well received, with hilarious catchphrases and characters including, Nan, Lauren and Derek.

LIVE AND KICKING. BBC Saturday morning show for kids. In 1993, Andi Peters, John Barrowman and Emma Forbes presented the show. There were several segments such as "Famous for Five Minutes", "It's My Life" and there would often be a musical guest and a cookery slot. In 1996, Zoe Ball and Jamie Theakston took over the presenter roles but sadly it came to an end in 2001.

LOUIS THEROUX'S WEIRD WEEKENDS. Louis Theroux is nerdy, awkward and hilarious, at the same time as being an amazing journalist and filmmaker. I love all things bizarre and abnormal and "Weird Weekends" is where Louis Theroux visits sub-cultures of America, spends time with them and immerses himself into their world. From the porn industry, to neo-nazis, the UFO obsessed, to wrestling. Louis Theroux does well at showing you all sides of s story. He gets involved without taking the mickey and the shows are just perfection. He could do a documentary about chopped tomatoes and I would still be like "THIS IS MENTAL".

LUNCHBOXES. It's a shame we couldn't get away with bringing a "Spiceworld" purple, plastic lunchbox to work nowadays. Or an orange "Action Man" one. Not so nice memories of school when the dinner ladies wouldn't let you leave if you hadn't eaten your lunch. Also, that infuriating feeling when you opened your lunchbox and your mum had given you an apple with some oat bar thing and your arch nemesis has got a DAIRYLEA LUNCHABLE. Choosing your lunchbox for school was a life changing decision. They were way kitsch-ier and tackier back in the day, plastic, perfectly square and I miss them.

M.

M.A.S.H. No, not the TV show, but the playground game that 90's kids were obsessed with. If you couldn't be bothered to origami a fortune teller you could predict your friend's future through a quick game of M.A.S.H. (Mansion, Apartment, Shed, House). By choosing a random number, your friend will discover their future property, spouse, job and number of children.

MADCHESTER. Madchester is a term for bands that came out of Manchester, in the late 80's, early 90's. These bands mixed alternative rock with elements of rave and 60's pop. Big bands in this scene were "The Stone Roses", "Happy Mondays", "The Charlatans" and "Inspiral Carpets".

MADE. MTV reality show that followed someone looking to completely transform their life. They were often teenagers with big dreams, such as wanting to be a boxing champion or a Rockstar etc. They would team up with professionals to help them achieve that goal and often they would do a performance or show off their new talent in some way.

MADELINE. Feature film based on the book series by Ludwig Bemelmans, about an orphan girl in Paris, trying to save her boarding school and home from closure. The casting was perfection, with the lead actress looking as close to the illustrations as you can get. You can kind of tell that the book wasn't really enough for a feature film, so there are some pretty random scenes that have been added in e.g. when the group of kids just stare at a couple kissing on a bench, strange.

MADONNA. Madonna carried on her pop queen reign all the way through the 90's and early 00's. She also starred in several movies during this time, most notably the musical "Evita". Us Brits adored Madonna, only 2 singles of hers released during the 90's charted outside the Top 10! Here are some of the best.

THE MADONNA PLAYLIST

1. VOGUE - 1990
2. JUSTIFY MY LOVE - 1990
3. RESCUE ME - 1991
4. EROTICA - 1992
5. DEEPER AND DEEPER - 1992
6. FEVER - 1993
7. RAIN - 1993
8. DON'T CRY FOR ME ARGENTINA - 1997
9. FROZEN - 1998
10. RAY OF LIGHT - 1998
11. BEAUTIFUL STRANGER - 1999
12. AMERICAN PIE - 2000
13. DON'T TELL ME - 2000
14. MUSIC - 2000

MAGIC KEY, THE. Book series that taught every 90's kid to read. Starring Biff, Chip and Kipper going on many magical adventures. They used to be categorised by reading levels in the school library. The year 1 kid that was on year 2 reading levels was held in high regard.

MAGIC SCHOOL BUS, THE. An animated TV series following the kooky Ms Frizzle and her class, as they go on field trips with a twist. Frizzle was quirky, had an interesting fashion sense and has become a feminist icon.

MALCOLM IN THE MIDDLE. American sitcom featuring Malcolm, the middle child, and his dysfunctional family. How Bryan Cranston went from playing the dad in this to one of the best villains of all time I shall never know. Another oldie that is just as funny today, watching it as an adult.

MANDELA, NELSON. The start of the most amazing decade also brought the emotional and long-awaited release of Nelson Mandela, after 27 hard years in prison. Mandela spent 18 years in the brutal Robben Island Prison with not even a bed or basic plumbing. The cell was tiny, he had to do hard labour, he could only receive one letter every 6 months and a 30-minute, face to face visit once a year. Nelson Mandela always remained the face of the South African anti-apartheid movement and when de Klerk became President, he ordered the release of Mandela. In 1993 Mandela and de Klerk were awarded the Nobel Peace Prize and a year later Mandela would be the new President of South Africa. He would remain president until his retirement from politics in 1999.

MANSON, MARILYN. Rock/metal singer famous for his gothic makeup and extreme attire. He released three albums that were very popular in his field "Antichrist Superstar" in 1996, "Mechanical Animals" in 1998 and "Holy Wood (In the Shadow of the Valley of Death)" in 2000. His biggest commercial success was the cover of "Tainted Love", released as the soundtrack to "Not Another Teen Movie" in 2001.

MAROON 5. In 2002 the world was introduced to Maroon 5 and their album "Songs About Jane". Every time you turned the radio on you would hear "This Love" or "She Will Be Loved". "Sunday Morning" was another banger from the album.

MARRIED WITH CHILDREN. Sitcom that began in the 80's it had more airtime in the 90's. Peggy Bundy is my spirit animal. Her fashion is so kitsch and her hair so big. Wife to Al Bundy, whose gormless expressions and idiocy brings so much laughter. Their two kids Kelly and Bud are equally hilarious, with Kelly being even dumber than Al and Bud thinking he's a god to all women. An amazing theme tune by the late, great Frank Sinatra, is an extra bonus to this hilarious sitcom.

MARS DELIGHT. The saddest loss to the chocolate aisle, the closest thing we have to it would be the Milky Way Crispy Rolls but it's not the same. Another discontinued Mars product was "Mars Planets". They were a bag of small chocolate balls, one was crispy, one soft and one chewy. They were similar to "Revels" but without the fear of accidentally getting a coffee one.

MARTIN, DEAN (1917-1995). Nicknamed "The King of Cool", Dean Martin was an entertainer, actor and singer. Famously part of the rat pack with Frank Sinatra, Sammy Davis Jnr, Peter Lawford and Joey Bishop. He began his showbiz career at 17, performing songs in local clubs. He met Jerry Lewis and the two formed a comedy double act, Dean Martin playing the straight man and Jerry Lewis the clown. After a successful radio show they made their TV debut in the 50's. They split up after 10 years due to creative differences and Martin resumed his singing career. He had several hit singles and began performing in Las Vegas, where he met and joined the Rat Pack. From there he starred in films and had his own TV show. Tragically Dean Martin passed away on Christmas day in 1995 when he was 78. He will always be remembered as the cool, calm and comedic crooner.

MARTIN, RICKY. We were in awe of this Latino man who suddenly popped up on our screens in the late 90's, with his raunchy single "Livin La Vida Loca". He had a second single "She Bangs" and then did a heartfelt duet with Christina Aguilera "Nobody Wants to be Lonely". He then totally vanished. It turned out he had a dab hand at acting too and went down this path after taking several years out to focus on his personal life.

MARTIN, STEVE. One of the best comedy actors of all time, Steve Martin brought us some awesome movies during the 90's/early 00's. His best of the period includes "Housesitter",

"Father of the Bride", "L.A Story", "Bowfinger" and "Cheaper by the Dozen".

MASSIVE ATTACK. Band from Bristol who made the genre of music "Trip-Hop" a thing. Top tracks include "Unfinished Sympathy", "Protection", "Risingson" and "Teardrop".

MATES, DATES SERIES. Teenage fiction by Cathy Hopkins. As a teenage female in the 90's/early 00's you surely would have at least checked "Mates, Dates and Inflatable Bras" out of the school library.

MATILDA. That scene with poor Boris and the chocolate cake, it used to make me break out in a cold sweat, so stressful. I reckon that's why I don't like chocolate cake to this day. Why was Miss Honey so unphased by Matilda's special powers? She was just like "Meh, just another day". A fantastic adaption of the Roald Dahl book and a must-see kids film for all the family to enjoy. The scene towards the beginning with Matilda making pancakes to that song by "Rusted Roots" is so satisfying.

MATRIX, THE. Movie that sees Keanu Reeves in his iconic role as Neo, an everyday computer hacker who comes into contact with a stranger. Essentially a techy drug dealer, the stranger offers Neo two pills. One pill to learn the reality of "The Matrix" or one pill to forget the entire conversation. And I will leave you to figure the rest out for yourself, partly because I don't want to spoil it, mostly because still don't get it. This movie made long leather coats and black glasses a look.

WHICH PILL WILL YOU TAKE?

MAX AND PADDY. "Road to Nowhere" is a hilarious mini series starring Peter Kay and Paddy McGuiness's characters from "Phoenix Nights". Max and Paddy are travelling round the UK in a motorhome. They are not the classiest of blokes and they get themselves into some hilarious situations. Paddy and Peter also released a comedy exercise video as Max and Paddy and that is also very funny.

MCDONALD'S BIRTHDAY PARTIES. Come on, every 90's kid has been to a birthday party at McDonalds! When I received an invitation for a McDonalds party, I RSVP'd quicker than Charlie's grandfather got out of bed when he got picked to go to the chocolate factory. If you were lucky the McDonald's mascots came out to join the party. Either way the parties were always good and the food top notch. Kids of today won't understand the anticipation of waiting to see whether any of the photos you took on your disposable camera came out ok.

MC HAMMER. The album from iconic rapper MC Hammer, "Please Hammer, Don't Hurt Em" dropped in 1990. The "You Can't Touch This" music vid with those pants! Everyone wanted harem pants after that. His next album "Too Legit to Quit" was bigger in the US than over here, but that big hit in 1990 was enough to earn him a place in our memories for life.

MEN BEHAVING BADLY. British sitcom following two mates who share a flat, drink too much beer, leer at women and behave badly in general. Tony and Gary singing "Sailing" in the pub in the episode, "Drunk", should happen every night in every pub. Another similar sitcom was "Game On", very underrated.

MERCURY, FREDDIE (1946-1991). The 90's brought the tragic passing of legendary music icon, Freddie Mercury. He was known for being one of the best performers of all time, as the lead singer of Queen. He knew how to put on a show and wow us with his amazing costumes, song writing and vocal ability. Freddie Mercury was born in Tanzania, his real name was Farrokh Bulsara and he went to boarding school in India. Due to conflict in Tanzania the family fled to London and during his college years he befriended several musicians. Freddie went on to form Queen in 1969. His iconic look and teeth were caused by him being born with 4 extra teeth; he didn't want them removed as he feared it would ruin his vocal ability. After playing their first gig in 1971, Queen soared in popularity. Even if you are not that familiar with the band, everyone knows "Bohemian Rhapsody". A true showman who brought the bottomless mic stand to the world. Queen and Freddie Mercury were deservedly enrolled into the Rock N Roll Hall of Fame in 2001.

MEYERS, NANCY. Director whose films contain a lot of house porn. She is still working her movie magic but some great films of hers to check out from this period are, "The Parent Trap", "Father of the Bride 1 & 2", "Something's Gotta Give" and "What Women Want".

MFI. British furniture shop that has closed its doors. The most boring place to be taken as a child, along with Homebase and Wickes. These were the places where dads were allowed to roam free with other dads. It got worse when they bumped into someone they knew and stood chatting for ages. Literal torture.

MICHAEL, GEORGE. Music legend and ex Wham lead singer, George Michael, carried on his solo success way into the 90's.

The music video for "Faith" was iconic, boy that man COULD move! Some other big hits for him during this time were "Don't Let the Sun Go Down On Me" with Elton John, "Fastlove", "Too Funky", "Jesus to a Child", "Spinning the Wheel" and "Outside".

MILKYBAR CHOO. Clearly the undying love of a nation wasn't enough to keep the "Milkybar Choo" from disappearing off our shelves. A chocolate bar that was a cross between a "Milky Bar" and fudge.

MINGLES. Variety box of mint chocolates by Benedicks that sadly became extinct in the 00's. When your mum and dad brought the box out it was the equivalent of that friend that never comes out, but when they do it's the best time.

MINICLIP. Online flash gaming website that is still going now, but was huge in the 00's. All school kids secretly ran it in the background of IT lessons. Popular games included "Club Penguin". Only true fans will remember the secret agent quiz, the calm before the storm right!? There was also "Bloons", "Heli Attack", "Taxi Gone Wild" and "Snowball Fight 3D".

MINIDISC. I feel like MiniDisc walked so the Sony Walkman could run. Could you actually get albums on this machine? I just remember them being blanks and you having to record on to them. You couldn't get accessories for them anywhere. Who said this was going to be the format of the future, honestly? I'm so sorry to those that were so invested they also brought the MiniDisc car stereo.

MINOGUE, KYLIE. How successful was Kylie during the 90's/early 00's!? She was everywhere! She was flawless and a true showgirl with endless hits. Everyone wanted a pair of gold hot pants after "Spinning Around".

KICKASS KYLIE PLAYLIST

1. TEARS ON MY PILLOW - 1990
2. BETTER THE DEVIL YOU KNOW - 1990
3. STEP BACK IN TIME - 1990
4. GIVE ME JUST A LITTLE MORE TIME - 1992
5. CONFIDE IN ME - 1994
6. SPINNING AROUND - 2000
7. ON A NIGHT LIKE THIS - 2000
8. KIDS FT ROBBIE WILLIAMS - 2000
9. CAN'T GET YOU OUT OF MY HEAD - KYLIE MINOGUE - 2001
10. IN YOUR EYES - 2002
11. LOVE AT FIRST SIGHT - 2002
12. COME INTO MY WORLD - 2002
13. SLOW - 2003

MISSY ELLIOTT. The mother of the adidas tracksuit and furry bucket hat, especially in baby blue and baby pink. She also suited a flat cap to a tee. Her song "Work It" had everyone confused with the lyrics. Turned out that confusing lyric was the previous line in reverse! Big hits for Missy in the early 00's was "Get Ur Freak On", "Work It", "Gossip Folks" and "Pass That Dutch".

MIS-TEEQ. British girl group consisting of Alesha Dixon, Su-Elise Nash and Sabrina Washington. Top songs include "Scandalous", "One Night Stand" and "All I Want". Alesha smashed it with those raps.

MIZZ. Magazine for teens that would always come with a free keyring or makeup. "CRINGE" was the best section of the mag, where you would feel for all those girls who fell over in front of their crush, or snot-bubbled on a date, so red faced. There were always flow charts and quizzes that would tell you if you were "a pulling pro" and if you answered mostly A's then he just was not that into you.

MOBY. Solo techno/pop musician. Most famous for songs like "Porcelain", "Natural Blues" and "Honey".

MOLOKO. Electronic/dance duo whose two biggest tunes were "Sing It Back" and "The Time is Now". Fun fact, the name "Moloko" was inspired by "The Clockwork Orange", the milk drink mixed with narcotics was called Moloko Plus. Moloko is close to the Russian for milk. Now you know.

MONA THE VAMPIRE. Animated TV show following a young vampire and her paranormal adventures. Everyday Halloween with Mona! Mona made vampires cool way before "Twilight".

MONSTER MUNCH. Not just any Monster Munch but the vanilla ice cream flavour that was limited edition. It was sweet instead of savoury, sugary instead of salty. Some loved and some loathed.

MOOD RING. Ring that changed colours depending on your mood, but really changed colours depending on the temperature of your finger. Truth hurts.

MORISSETTE, ALANIS. Alanis Morissette was a female, Canadian badass! She released the album "Jagged Little Pill" in 1995 with hits including the ultimate angry anthem "You Oughta Know". And let's not forget the not so ironic, "Ironic" and "Hand in My Pocket". Two years later she released the single "Thank U", with a very memorable music video.

MOTHER THERESA (1910-1997). "Let us always meet each other with a smile, for a smile is the beginning of love". Beautiful words from a beautiful soul. Mother Theresa was a famous nun and missionary who gave her life to helping others. She's one of the greatest humanitarians of the 20th Century and was made a Saint in 2016. She gave her life to looking after the sick and poor. "If we really want to love, we must learn how to forgive".

MOULIN ROUGE. Fab musical directed by the brilliant Baz Luhrmann. Nicole Kidman and Ewan McGregor are brilliant in their lead roles, such chemistry between them! And Nicole Kidman looks so spicy in those amazing showgirl outfits. The way the movie takes modern songs and turns them into musical numbers works so well with the theme of the movie. Get the tissues ready, an ugly cry could be imminent at the end.

MOUSEHUNT. A slapstick, child friendly comedy caper starring Lee Evans and Nathan Lane, chasing a mouse who refuses to leave their newly inherited mansion. "Home Alone" esque but Kevin McAllister is a mouse.

MR BEAN. Sitcom that should have had more seasons than 1! Mr Bean is played by a British comedy legend, Rowan Atkinson. His facial expressions are incredible, I've never seen a man whose face is so much like Playdoh. The theme music was very depressing considering the show was not at all. There's been an animated series and films since. Mr Bean taught us to enjoy our own company and be content with our own selves. You don't need others to make you happy. Every girl wants a man to look at her like Mr Bean looks at Teddy.

MR FREEZE. Ice pops that looked like long sticks. Mr Freeze pops came in a variety of flavours and were the ones you got at the shops with your friends for like 50p.

MRS DOUBTFIRE. Potentially the best family film of all time. Hilarious and heart-warming movie starring Robin Williams. He plays a newly divorced parent who is desperate to spend time with his children, but sadly has lost custody. So, he does what any normal father would do in this situation and disguises himself as a woman, getting himself hired as their nanny. Robin Williams's makeup took 4 hours every day to do. Madness! This film has so many fantastic scenes, Robin Williams is one of the funniest people to have graced this planet. The ending is super emotional and hits you right where it hurts.

MSN MESSENGER. A vital part of teenage life, where friendships were made, and hearts were broken. So many hours were spent waiting for your crush's display name to pop up in the right-hand corner. Everyone had a love heart with either their boyfriend/girlfriend or best friend's name as part of their screen name. Statuses often contained meaningful song lyrics, you could let people know you were sad by changing the lyrics to something deep and depressing. Then when you would get asked if you're ok, you would just say you were fine, but obviously you were not. Choosing a display picture was serious business and those nudges and winks were the most annoying thing on the planet. Appearing offline and doing some casual cyber stalking, then switching to online so your crush got a notification, you know because they must have missed you the first time. Even more painful was when you saw someone was typing, so you stopped typing, then you waited and then THEY stopped typing so you never got that message. And the worst, when you had to end your conversation because your mum needed to use the phone, oh, the rage. The hilarity of all of this was you spent all day with these people at school and you then rushed home to chat to them even more!

MULHOLLAND DRIVE. It's sexy, it's stylish, it's surreal. A David Lynch masterpiece about Rita who has amnesia and Betty, an actress. They go on the hunt for clues to find out what really happened in Rita's accident and find her true identity. It's one massive mind boggle, a truly unique movie.

MUNIZ, FRANKIE. Child actor of the 90's/early 00's known mostly for his starring role as Malcolm in "Malcolm in the Middle". Other roles were more in movies, including "My Dog Skip", "Big Fat Liar" and "Agent Cody Banks". He also played a totally random part as Cher's boyfriend in "Stuck on You".

MURPHY, EDDIE. He may not always be pumping out unforgettable movies, but when Eddie Murphy is at his best, it's hard to find better. His best releases in this era include "Boomerang", "The Nutty Professor", "Mulan", "Dr Dolittle", "Bowfinger", "Life" and "Shrek".

MURRAY, BILL. Another comedy legend, Bill Murray, has to be in everyone's top 10. He starred in so many great films during this era. The best includes "Groundhog Day", "Ed Wood", "Kingpin", "Space Jam", "Rushmore" and "Lost in Translation".

MUSIC VIDEOS. They just don't make music videos like they used to anymore. Here are some memorable videos from the era.

ICONIC MUSIC VIDEOS OF THE 90S/EARLY 00S

1. FREEDOM - GEORGE MICHAEL - 1990
2. NOTHING COMPARES TO YOU - SINEAD O'CONNOR - 1990
3. BLACK HOLE SUN - SOUNDGARDEN - 1994
4. SABOTAGE - BEASTIE BOYS - 1994
5. FIRESTARTER - THE PRODIGY - 1996
6. ROLLERCOASTER - RED HOT CHILLI PEPPERS - 1996
7. WANNABE - SPICE GIRLS - 1996
8. AROUND THE WORLD - DAFT PUNK - 1997
9. BITTERSWEET SYMPHONY - THE VERVE - 1997
10. COME TO DADDY - APHEX TWIN - 1997
11. EVERLONG - FOO FIGHTERS - 1997
12. KARMA POLICE - RADIOHEAD - 1997
13. MAN I FEEL LIKE A WOMAN - SHANIA TWAIN - 1997
14. NO SURPRISES - RADIOHEAD - 1997
15. THAT DON'T IMPRESS ME MUCH - SHANIA TWAIN - 1997
16. VIVA FOREVER - SPICE GIRLS - 1997
17. HIT ME BABY ONE MORE TIME - BRITNEY SPEARS - 1998
18. PRAISE YOU - FATBOY SLIM - 1998
19. CALIFORNICATION - RED HOT CHILLI PEPPERS - 1999
20. COFFEE AND TV - BLUR - 1999
21. HEY BOY, HEY GIRL - CHEMICAL BROTHERS - 1999
22. LEARN TO FLY - FOO FIGHTERS - 1999
23. MAMMALS - BLOODHOUND GANG - 1999
24. MY NAME IS - EMINEM - 1999
25. NATURAL BLUES - MOBY - 1999
26. RIGHT HERE, RIGHT NOW - FATBOY SLIM - 1999
27. FIRST DATE - BLINK 182 - 2001
28. WEAPON OF CHOICE - FATBOY SLIM - 2001
29. WHERE'S YOUR HEAD AT - BASEMENT JAXX - 2001
30. VIRTUAL INSANITY - JAMIROQUAI - 2002

MUZZY. Anyone who had French lessons in the 90's/early 00's surely must remember Muzzy! God knows what Muzzy actually was. Monster? Yeti? Bear? No one knows.

MY FAMILY. One of Britain's best loved sitcoms began in 2000. British legend Robert Lindsay played Ben Harper, head of the household, who works as a dentist. Zoe Wanamaker, Kris Marshall, Daniela Denby-Ashe and Gabriel Thomson are the perfect supporting cast, with each one bringing something different to their characters. Ben has a very cynical sense of humour and finds himself in some hilarious, sticky situations.

MY HERO. British sitcom starring Ardal O'Hanlon as Thermoman, a superhero who is trying to hide his powers and fit into standard earth life. The acting is very believable considering the storyline is very UNbelievable. The show doesn't need a lot of brain power to watch, but what's wrong with giving your brain a rest and just having a good old-fashioned laugh.

MY KIND OF MUSIC. As a huge music lover this was one of the best game shows ever in the history of TV. Hosted by 90's game show fav Michael Barrymore, where all the rounds tested a contestant's music knowledge. Barrymore was huge in the 90's, presenting other popular shows such as "Strike it Lucky" and "My Kind of People".

MY PARENTS ARE ALIENS. Children's TV show where aliens Brian and Sophie Johnson live on earth and adopt three orphan siblings, in hopes to give them a better life. Sophie was a ditzy, blonde character for two series and then out of the blue pops up this redhead actress, playing exactly the same character, and everyone was like what the hell happened!? They gave some reason in the third series that she wasn't able to morph back to her original self or something. Still an amazing series for kids and to be fair the new Sophie did just as good of a job.

MY SCENE. Fashion dolls, similar to Barbie in body but with bigger heads. Total style icons back in the day.

MYSPACE AND BEBO. THE social media sites to be on in the early 00's. When you wanted to be petty so you would re-shuffle your top friends on MySpace, to show people they had to earn their spot in your top 10. That bottom row was the danger zone. When you first joined Myspace and "Tom" was auto your friend and for a while you couldn't work out who he was and why he was spying on your page. Spending hours deciding what song sends out the best message for who you are as a person, so people feel like they know you when they visit your page. From there you would switch sites to Bebo, spending the next hour customising your skin and deciding who to give your precious "luv" to. Some friends would have "Piczo" websites as well and they would get image inspo from Bebo skins, the tackier and glitterier the better. I wish the biggest problem in life was still deciding who to give your days' worth of luv too.

MY SUPER SWEET SIXTEEN. Reality TV show on MTV about rich kids who had no shame showing off how spoiled they were on TV. These parties were more extravagant than weddings. There would often be a celeb casually performing and always a car, worth more than a small house, as a gift. I often found myself wondering how many friends of theirs were actual friends and how many just knew they threw the sickest of parties.

MY WIFE AND KIDS. US sitcom with the coolest of TV parents. Damon Wayans plays dad, Michael Kyle. He often took the mickey out of his kids but was always right by their side no matter what crazy stuff they'd get up to.

N.

NAKED CHEF, THE. Jamie Oliver, one of Britain's best loved chefs, with his cookbooks outselling Harry Potter at one stage! Back in 1999 when "The Naked Chef" first aired, Jamie was a humble sous chef, flying around London on his scooter. His motto was "food had to be a laugh". He also explained he wasn't the naked one, but the food was. Jamie introduced a stripped back style of cooking, throwing a bit of oil here, scattering herbs there. Measurements? What are those? Simple. Home. Cooking.

NELLY. Everyone has got to know the words to "Hot in Herre". This was a jam and got everyone on the floor at school discos. We loved this rapper when he came on the scene with his grillz, sweatband and face plaster. Hits included "Country Grammar", "E.I", "Ride Wit Me" and "Dilemma" ft Kelly Rowland.

NEOPETS. A virtual pet website where you could use virtual currency to buy virtual items for your virtual pets. Fans of Neopets will remember such pets as "JubJub", "Acara" and "Chia". How greedy were those things, you would try and feed them a veggie and they would be like "no thnx". IF YOU WERE THAT HUNGRY YOU'D EAT IT. Guilds were too cliquey for me and I wasn't about that life. Sorry to those that didn't play Neopets and have no idea what they've just read.

N.E.R.D. A band that was a hip hop and rock crossover, famously fronted by Pharrell Williams. They released bangers in the early 00's such as, "Lapdance", "Rockstar" and "She Wants to Move".

NEVER MIND THE BUZZCOCKS. Music and comedy quiz show. During the early days, the show was presented by Mark Lamarr, with captains Phill Jupitus and Sean Hughes. Simon Anstell took over from Mark Lamarr but this was a lot later in the 00's. The best rounds were the intros and the identity parades.

NINTENDO. In 1991 we had the "SNES" which was awesome but the painful blisters you used to get from the D-Pad were too real. This was followed by "Nintendo 64" in 1996. We said hello to "Gamecube" in 2001 and of course the Gameboy. Nintendo have brought us so many incredible games over the years and in the 90's they really found their feet in the gaming world. The games below broke up even the strongest of friendships.

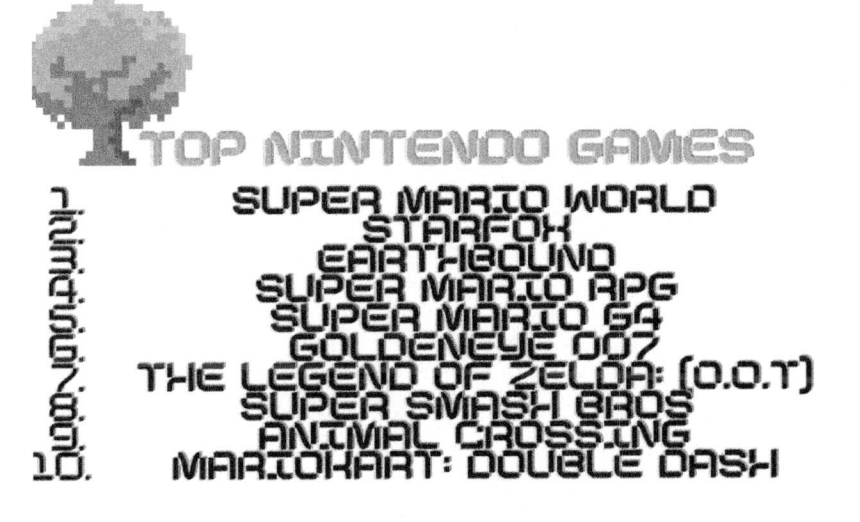

TOP NINTENDO GAMES

1. SUPER MARIO WORLD
2. STARFOX
3. EARTHBOUND
4. SUPER MARIO RPG
5. SUPER MARIO 64
6. GOLDENEYE 007
7. THE LEGEND OF ZELDA: (O.O.T)
8. SUPER SMASH BROS
9. ANIMAL CROSSING
10. MARIOKART: DOUBLE DASH

NOEL'S HOUSE PARTY. I'm talking Noel Edmonds and Mr Blobby in a fake house, in the fictional village of Crinkley Bottom. Knock, Knock. Who's there? Noel never knew until he opened that door and then SURPRISE. Whoever it was, it was always going to be a fun Saturday evening filled with immature humor. "Gotcha" was the original "Punk'd", a hidden camera prank on celebrities. "NTV" was the first time hidden cameras were put in the homes of unsuspecting members of the public. Sorry Ant and Dec but Noel did it first. I think a revival is in order, don't you?

NOKIA 3310/3410. Any 90's kid's first ever mobile. My mum still uses mine to this day so they have staying power. Actually I think the battery lasted a whole week without a charge! "Snake" was the best time filler but very intense. When that snake got faster and faster your sweat levels increased more and more. That Nokia jingle that played when you turned the phone on, one of the most nostalgic sounds you can get.

NOTORIOUS B.I.G (1972-1997). Also known as Biggie Smalls. American rapper that some would argue is the best rapper of all time. Sadly he was wrapped up (actually no pun intended here!) in the dark side of the rap world and was taken from us too early. "Juicy", "Mo Money Mo Problems" and "Hypnotize" are three classic rap tunes. Close friends with P.Diddy, P.Diddy released "I'll be Missing You" along with B.I.G's then girlfriend Faith Evans in memoriam. A few years after his death "Nasty Girl" was released by a collection of rappers in his honour, another great song and a great tribute to B.I.G.

NOVELTY PHONES. How many movies have you seen where they have the coolest bedroom phone? There was the American Football phone, by "Sports Illustrated" in 1991. The Karma Chameleon phone that BT featured in their ad in 2002. Barbie phone and "Dream Phone" were popular phone toys but not actual phones. There was a Bart Simpson themed landline and a Homer one sitting on the couch. Classics like the hamburger and lips were actually 80's but still widely used during the 90's.

NOVELTY SONGS. The 90's/early 00's were a haven for novelty songs. Some of them were really, really weird. Love them or hate them, you have to admit these songs are part of your life's soundtrack. Seriously, if you're not going to get excited when any of these come on at a wedding reception, why even go?

NOVELTY SONGS OF THE 90'S/EARLY 00'S

1. ITSY BITSY TEENIE WEENIE - BOMBALURINA - 1990
2. I'M TOO SEXY - RIGHT SAID FRED - 1992
3. MACARENA - LOS DEL RIO - 1993
4. COTTON EYED JOE - REDNEX - 1995
5. SCATMAN - SCATMAN JOHN - 1995
6. SEX ON THE BEACH - T-SPOON - 1997
7. TUBTHUMPING - CHUMBAWUMBA - 1997
8. HORNY - MOUSSE T VS HOT N JUICY - 1998
9. TEQUILA - TERRORVISION - 1998
10. WITCH DOCTOR - CARTOONS - 1998
11. BLUE - EIFFEL 65 - 1999
12. BECAUSE I GOT HIGH - AFROMAN - 2000
13. HEY BABY - DJ OTZI - 2000
14. OH STICK YOU - DAPHNE AND CELESTE - 2000
15. THE HAMPSTER DANCE SONG - HAMPTON THE HAMPSTER - 2000
16. THE WHISTLE SONG - DJ ALIGATOR PROJECT - 2000
17. WHO LET THE DOGS OUT? - THE BAHA MEN - 2000
18. LITTLE YELLOW FISH - LITTLE TREES - 2001
19. CHIHUAHUA - DJ BOBO - 2002
20. THE KETCHUP SONG - LAS KETCHUP - 2002
21. THE CHEEKY SONG - CHEEKY GIRLS - 2003
22. THE FAST FOOD SONG - FAST FOOD ROCKERS - 2003
23. GAY BAR - ELECTRIC SIX - 2003
24. NUMA NUMA - O-ZONE - 2003

NOW THAT'S WHAT I CALL MUSIC. "I don't want to spend my pocket money on a NOW album" said no 90's kid ever. These compilations were so popular during this period. The first half of both A and B sides were awesome and then the second half were like the songs you kind of heard of but not really.

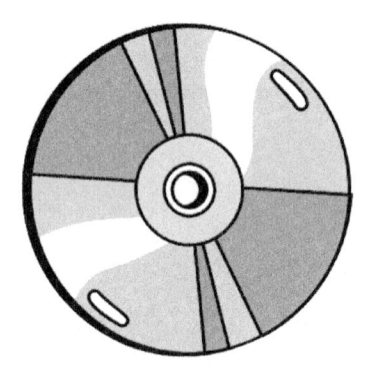

NSTORM. Video game creators that you have to thank for classic internet games such as "Elf Bowling" and various spin-offs, "Frogapult" and "Chicken Archery". These games were so good to play free online, not so sure about buying them for the Nintendo though.

NSYNC. Boy band made up of Justin Timberlake, JC Chasez, Chris Kirkpatrick, Joey Fatone and Lance Bass. The princes of the frosted tip. Top songs include "Bye Bye Bye", "Pop", "It's Gonna Be Me", "Girlfriend" ft Nelly and "Tearin Up My Heart". Notable hits by Justin Timberlake when he went solo were "Like I Love You", "Senorita", "Cry Me a River" and "Rock Your Body".

O.

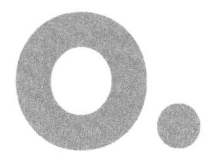

OAKIE DOKE. Stop motion animation about an acorn man who takes pleasure in helping his fellow woodland brothers out. #BEMOREOAKIEDOKE

OASIS. I was asked to stop singing "Wonderwall". I said maybe. The kings of the Brit-Pop scene, along with Blur. One of the best bands in the universe, it's impossible to do a playlist as every song's a winner. The albums you must hear from start to finish, released between the 90's and 2002 are "Definitely Maybe", "What's the Story Morning Glory", "Be Here Now", "Standing on the Shoulders of Giants" and "Heathen Chemistry".

OFFICE, THE. Popular British sitcom/mockumentary created by Ricky Gervais and Stephen Merchant, also starring Ricky Gervais as the famous David Brent. This show is as cringe as when you ask someone how they are more than once by mistake. David Brent is the guy that takes everything too far. He has his own version of political correctness but never intends to offend. He is so delusional with no off switch. All the other characters are funny too, Gareth being a kiss-arse and Tim with his facial expressions that speak louder than words. Tim and Dawn, the best love story of the 21st Century.

OLD BEAR STORIES. Collection of stories by Jane Hissey, paired with beautiful illustrations. A stop-motion animated TV series was created and was so good it ended up winning a BAFTA.

OLSEN TWINS, THE. Mary-Kate and Ashley Olsen, who can forget! Probably the most famous twins. They first started off in "Full House" in the late 80's. Their next biggest show was "Two of a Kind" in the late 90's. They also starred in films such as "It Takes Two", "Passport to Paris", "Switching Goals", "Our Lips Are Sealed", "Winning London", "Holiday in the Sun" and "New York Minute".

ONE FOOT IN THE GRAVE. British sitcom whose main character, Victor Meldrew, is the moodiest, moaniest and unluckiest man, who just wants to enjoy his retirement in peace. It brought something different to other sitcoms around at the time, as well as being hilarious.

ONE HIT WONDERS. The 90's/early 00's produced a lot of one hit wonders, some amazing, some questionable. It's quite a loose term "one hit wonder" and different people have different interpretations of its meaning. For me, I have listed below any artist that has only had one very successful hit; they may have had other hits, but nowhere near the heights of their first.

ERA DEFINING ONE HIT WONDERS

1. GROOVE IS IN THE HEART - DEEE-LITE - 1990
2. I TOUCH MYSELF - THE DIVINYLS - 1990
3. THERE SHE GOES - THE LA'S - 1990
4. WHAT'S UP - 4 NON BLONDES - 1993
5. SATURDAY NIGHT - WIGFIELD
6. YOU AND ME - THE WANNADIES - 1994
7. BREAKFAST AT TIFFANYS - DEEP BLUE SOMETHING - 1995
8. YOU'RE GORGEOUS - BABYBIRD - 1996
9. BITCH - MEREDITH BROOKS - 1997
10. CRUSH - JENNIFER PAIGE - 1998
11. DANCE THE NIGHT AWAY - THE MAVERICKS - 1998
12. KING OF MY CASTLE - WAMDUE PROJECT - 1998
13. ONLY GET WHAT YOU GIVE - THE NEW RADICALS - 1998
14. BREATHE AGAIN - ADAM RICKITT - 1999
15. DON'T CALL ME BABY - MADISON AVENUE - 1999
16. I QUIT - HEPBURN - 1999
17. MAMBO NO.5 - LOU BEGA - 1999
18. STEAL MY SUNSHINE - LEN - 1999
19. THONG SONG - SISQO - 1999
20. AIRHEAD - GIRLS@PLAY - 2000
21. NO MORE - 3LW - 2000
22. HE LOVES U NOT - DREAM - 2001
23. RAPTURE - IIO - 2001
24. WHEREVER YOU WILL GO - THE CALLING - 2001
25. 1000 MILES - VANESSA CARLTON - 2001
26. MOVE YOUR FEET - JUNIOR SENIOR - 2002
27. MY NECK, MY BACK - KHIA - 2002
28. CHOOZA LOOZA - MARIA WILLSON - 2003
29. MISFIT - AMY STUDT - 2003
30. ROC YA BODY - MVP - 2003
31. UH OH - LUMIDEE - 2003
32. LET ME LOVE YOU - MARIO - 2004
33. MOVE YA BODY - NINA SKY - 2004

ONLY FOOLS AND HORSES. I know, I know, Only Fools was an 80's programme but the Christmas specials in the 90's contained some of the best moments in TV history. Especially, the 1996 Christmas trio. The hilarious Batman and Robin sketch, the watch, so many moments that I just don't want to spoil for you if you haven't seen them. They came back in 2001, 2002 and 2003 with Christmas specials, all amazing. You can see why the UK often choose this show as the best sitcom ever.

OPAL FRUITS. The name change from "Opal Fruits" to "Starburst" was headline news in the 90's. The change was due to the sweets being called "Starburst" in the US, Mars decided to change them in the UK, so they matched. The only difference was that "Starburst" had a blackcurrant sweet and a lemon and lime sweet. "Opal Fruits" had a lemon sweet and lime sweet separate, no blackcurrant. I was so lazy that if I opened the wrapper and paper was still on the sweet, I just ate paper.

OSBOURNES, THE. Before the Kardashian's there was the Osbournes, the founding family of reality TV. Ozzy and Sharon starred with their kids Kelly and Jack, Aimee Osbourne wanted no part in the show. It was basically 45 minutes of arguing but you couldn't help but tune in. Kelly had a short-lived singing career, she sang the Black Sabbath classic with her dad, "Changes" in 2003. The year before she released a version of "Papa Don't Preach" and "Shut Up". Ozzy Osbourne just had such a way with words, "Life has a way of kicking you in the f***ing nuts". Poetic.

OTIS THE AARDVARK. A puppet presenter on CBBC from 1994-1995 and a forgotten TV hero. He used to present the links on BBC alongside a human presenter. You knew to never question a talking aardvark.

O-TOWN. Early 00's boy band with two killer songs "Liquid Dreams" and emotional ballad that spoke to us in our youth, "All or Nothing". Cue cheesy boy band fist drop.

OUTDOOR CHILDHOODS. Where have they gone? Me and my fellow 90's kids were out playing all the time, be it with the kids in the neighbourhood or school friends. Our parents had a hard time getting us to come in for dinner, now parents have a hard time getting their children to go outside! I remember winter days playing out and you'd hear the occasional ice cream van. You'd be thinking, no one wants an ice-cream right now, it's freezing, read the room Mr Whippy! The cars used to honk their horns because we would block the road playing sports. Too sad that the world has come to this.

OUTKAST. Hip-hop duo, Big Boi and Andre 3000. Awesome songs released in the 00's was "Ms Jackson", "So Fresh and Clean", "Hey Ya" and "Roses". How much of a tune was "Hey

Ya"? A school disco floor filler, pre-adolescents shaking it like a polaroid picture.

OVERHEAD PROJECTOR. Who remembers being asked to put the acetate on the projector during school and feeling the sweet warmth hit you like stepping out off a plane on holiday? And the person sitting next to it making shadow figures when the teacher wasn't looking. What a rebel.

OWL BABIES. I'm sorry but have you actually seen what a baby owl looks like!? Seriously, I think anyone that thinks they've seen aliens has actually just seen a baby owl. This children's book was a classic for any kid growing up in the 90's, beautiful illustrations by Patrick Benson and wonderfully written by Martin Waddell.

P.

PANDA POPS. The WKD for children. Every kid got a sugar high from one of these drinks, commonly served at birthday parties. Panda Pops and party rings were a recipe for disaster when you're a mum or dad in charge of 10 kids at a soft play centre. These drinks remind me of party bags you used to get from your friend's birthday parties. Also included in these bags would often be sweets, balloons, a party hat, a piece of birthday cake, a transfer tattoo and if your friend's mum was really trying to impress, a small toy.

PARTRIDGE, ALAN. I used to think Alan Partridge was a real person. Embarrassing, I know. Turns out a guy called Steve Coogan, created and plays Alan Partridge. His first big show as Partridge was "Knowing Me Knowing You", where the famous catchphrase "AH HAH!" came from. Alan is a talk show host and interviews people... Badly. Then he went on to do "I'm Alan Partridge". This is where Alan is now a DJ, kind of failing at life. It's totally hilarious, so much so, my husband can't hold a conversation without dropping a Partridge reference. Alan is very harsh to his assistant Lynn, and he must hog the limelight all the time. Alan has an unhealthy addiction to Toblerone and I know how he feels as I am a recovering Choc Digestive addict.

PAUL, SEAN. Most of Sean Paul's hits blessed us later in the 00's but in 2002/2003 it all began with "Get Busy", "Gimme the Light" and "Like Glue". At this time, anything with Sean Paul in it was a total hit. He featured in "Baby Boy" with Beyonce and "Breathe" with Blu Cantrell. All hail the lord of the dance..hall!

PECK, GREGORY (1916-2003). Incredible actor who famously played Atticus Finch in "To Kill a Mockingbird". A super stylish and suave man, he also stole our hearts and Audrey Hepburn's in "Roman Holiday". Other roles he is remembered for are "The Omen" and also "Cape Fear" in the 60's. He sadly passed away from a form of pneumonia aged 87 but his movies and legacy live on.

PEPPER ANN. Animated tv show about Pepper Ann and her friends in middle school. Watching it back as an adult, Pepper Ann is pretty feminist. She kicked the female stereotype out of the window and paved the way for other bad-ass female characters like Eliza from "The Wild Thornberrys".

PERCY THE PARK KEEPER. Main character of the beloved Nick Butterworth books, following Percy and his life looking after the animals in the park. The always needed his help with one thing or another so he was a busy man. The TV series was also a success.

PET RESCUE. Shield the eyes of your dogs and cats, they don't need to see their fellow pets in such states. British daytime TV show about pets being rescued from various traumatic situations, cared for and either re-homed or put back into the wild. An emotional rollercoaster with a very nostalgic theme tune. Another similar programme at the time was "Animal Hospital".

PHOENIX NIGHTS. Sitcom co-created by and starring Peter Kay as Brian Potter, a failed club owner who was hoping to strike it lucky with his third attempt. "Phoenix Nights" is set in a Northern club that claims to offer "entertainment". Max and Paddy are the club's doormen and they bagged their own spin off series.

PHOENIX, RIVER (1970-1993). Very tragic loss at such a young age. River Phoenix was an American actor towards the start of his career. He featured in films such as "Stand By Me", "Indiana Jones and the Last Crusade" and "My Own Private Idaho". River Phoenix sadly died of a drug overdose whilst at The Viper Room in LA. So much potential that we sadly didn't get to see.

PIGGIN' PIGS. Collectable, humorous pig figurines that at least one person in your family owned. Often seen on the shelves of charity shops.

PIMP MY RIDE. Popular MTV show hosted by Xzibit. X would meet people whose cars were so run down they had like a door hanging off and only 3 wheels. He'd take it to the legends at "West Coast Customs" and they would totally transform it. The owner of the car would be surprised at the end with what they'd done. It was always mental and quite often tacky as hell (I'm talking flames stencilled up the side of the car type of thing). They would always have crazy speakers and about four TVs in the boot. Totally unnecessary but why not.

PINGU. We all tried to make a plasticine figure of this little guy. Pingu was one of the best kids shows ever with his angry expression and noot noots. The show actually began in 1986 but ran the whole way through the 90's and early 00's. I definitely see parts of my adult self in Pingu.

PINK. Pink totally slayed the pop world in the early 00's. Her album "Mizundastood" was the soundtrack to many a teenage girl's life. Before this album she released "There You Go" and "You Make Me Sick", they had a bit more of a hip-hop vibe. She was also part of the collab of the century "Lady Marmalade" with Christina Aguilera, Mya, Lil Kim and Missy Elliott. In 2003 she released her next successful album, "Try This" which was equally as amazing.

PINKY AND THE BRAIN. Animated TV series about a genius mouse and his not so genius sidekick, trying to take over the world each day. Spin off from "Animaniacs".

PIPER, BILLIE. You may know Billie Piper as an actress, but the world needs to know she started off as a popstar. She released two good albums including singles "Because We Want To", "Honey to the Bee" and "Day and Night". She dropped this bombshell in 2003 that she would be retiring from music. We were all so sad, but then she popped back on our screen acting and all that sadness washed away.

PLATFORM SANDALS. Steve Madden was famous for his platform sandal in the 90's. They screamed summertime grunge.

PLAY DAYS. Educational TV show for pre-schoolers, with characters including "Why Bird", "Peggy Patch" and "Poppy".

PLAYSTATION. Sony first introduced the UK to the PS1 in 1995, with the PS2 being released in 2000. The excitement when your friend got the latest console, only to find out they only have one controller. We all loved gaming so much that we overloaded our extension cable with so many plugs and risked setting our houses on fire. Can you believe there was only 1mb of memory on each memory card! No wonder everyone had a folder of the things.

MOST MEMORABLE PS1 AND PS2 GAMES

1. STREET RACER - 1994
2. WIPEOUT - 1995
3. INTERNATIONAL TRACK AND FIELD - 1996
4. CASTLEVANIA: SYMPHONY OF THE NIGHT - 1997
5. GRAND THEFT AUTO/VICE CITY/SAN ANDREAS - 1997/2002/2004
6. GRAN TURISMO 2/4 - 1997/2004
7. MICRO MACHINES V3 - 1997
8. ODDWORLD: ABE'S ODDYSEE - 1997
9. TEKKEN 3 - 1997
10. METAL GEAR SOLID - 1998
11. RESIDENT EVIL 2 - 1998
12. DINO CRISIS - 1999
13. FINAL FANTASY VIII/X - 1999/2001
14. ISS PRO-EVOLUTION SOCCER - 1999
15. SILENT HILL 1/2 - 1999/2001
16. DEAD OR ALIVE 2 - 2000
17. TONY HAWKS PRO SKATER 2 - 2000
18. DEVIL MAY CRY - 2001
19. MAX PAYNE - 2001
20. KINGDOM HEARTS - 2002
21. MANHUNT - 2003
22. PRINCE OF PERSIA - 2003
23. HITMAN - 2004
24. KILLZONE - 2004

POGS. I am honoured to be married to a former Pogs champion. Also known as "Milk Caps", Pogs was a popular playground game in the early to mid-90's. I would go as far as to say Pogs were playground currency. They taught you the hustle. No doubt you worked your butt off building the sickest Pogs collection only to find your mum or dad threw them away ten years later. Your life's work gone! I was one of those kids that had Pogs but didn't know why.

POKEMON. Known as "pocket monsters" in Japan. Pokemon is a TV series, with feature films, oodles of merchandise and video games. It has grown to be one of the bestselling franchises. Pokemon cards were all the rage and we used to have a special folder for them, arranged to perfection. No one could take away the thrill you got from opening a brand-new packet of Pokemon cards. When someone got a card in Asian writing and we all thought it was super rare and they had struck gold. There was actually a game you were meant to play with the cards, but I was all about the thrill of the hunt.

POLKA DOT SHORTS. Canadian TV show for young children, with a catchy as hell theme tune. IMDB's description of this show is "The documentation of a collection of beings whose existences seem to revolve almost exclusively around the discovery of a single pair of dot patterned under apparel." If that hasn't sold it to you, I don't know what will.

POLLY POCKET. Another toy we thought if we kept in pristine condition it could make us a mint. A small locket that once opened reveals this whole little world with tiny dolls to match. There was a boy version too, "Mighty Max", which was slightly horror themed. Polly branched into larger fashion dolls and "Fashion Polly" was born. You could buy little rubber outfits and mix and match them to create your own looks.

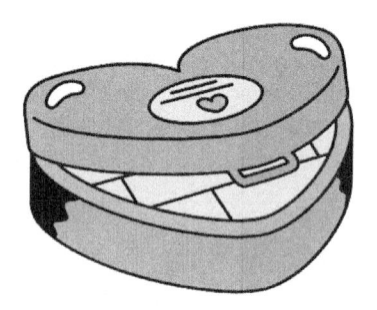

POO-CHI. This toy made you feel you were well 21st century. One of the first robo-pet toys, Poo-Chi was a robotic dog that was sadly discontinued two years after its release in 2000.

POP IDOL. The UK's first singing talent contest producing talents such as Will Young and Gareth Gates. You thought you weren't into these shows yet somehow you still found yourself getting irate when someone you liked got voted out. Another popular singing contest "Popstars: The Rivals", the winner of that show was "Girls Aloud". These shows made us believe that being a huge popstar was totally within our reach.

POP MUSIC. Hello my fellow pop-timists. Tell me these songs weren't bangers in their own right.

POP PLAYLIST

1. HOLD ON - WILSON PHILLIPS - 1990
2. I AM THE ONE AND ONLY - CHESNEY HAWKES - 1991
3. MR LOVERMAN - SHABBA RANKS - 1991
4. ACHY BREAKY HEART - BILLY RAY CYRUS - 1992
5. MOVIN ON UP - M PEOPLE - 1993
6. MR VAIN - CULTURE BEAT - 1993
7. I SWEAR - ALL-4-ONE - 1994
8. YOU GOTTA BE - DES'REE - 1994
9. OOH AHH - GINA G - 1996
10. FREE - ULTRANATE - 1997
11. KISS ME - SIXPENCE NONE THE RICHER - 1997
12. THE ONLY ONE - ETERNAL - 1997
13. THINGS CAN ONLY GET BETTER - D:REAM - 1997
14. YOU MIGHT NEED SOMEBODY - SHOLA AMA - 1997
15. YOUR WOMAN - WHITE TOWN - 1997
16. ADDICTED TO BASS - PURETONE - 1998
17. DIFFERENT SIZES - BEAUTIFUL SOUTH - 1998
18. OH LA LA - THE WISEGUYS - 1998
19. STRANDED - LUTRICIA MCNEAL - 1998
20. WHEN YOU'RE GONE - BRYAN ADAMS FT MEL C - 1998
21. BACK HERE - BBMACK - 1999
22. EVERY MORNING - SUGAR RAY - 1999
23. GIRL ON TV - LFO - 1999
24. I TRY - MACY GRAY - 1999
25. MARIA - BLONDIE - 1999
26. (MUCHO MAMBO) SWAY - SHAFT - 1999
27. SMOOTH - SANTANA FT ROB THOMAS - 1999
28. VIVA LA RADIO - LOLLY - 1999
29. PUSH IT ALL ASIDE - ALISHA'S ATTIC - 2000
30. DROPS OF JUPITER - TRAIN - 2001
31. BORN TO TRY - DELTA GOODREM - 2002
32. KISS KISS - HOLLY VALANCE - 2002
33. MORE TO LIFE - STACIE ORRICO - 2003
34. SO YESTERDAY - HILARY DUFF - 2003
35. STUCK - STACIE ORRICO - 2003
36. SUPERSTAR - JAMELIA - 2003
37. BABY CAKES - 3 OF A KIND - 2004
38. DUMB - 411 - 2004

POP PUNK. Why did we all think we were so punk rock just because we listened to "Good Charlotte" and "Simple Plan"? Some amazing pop punk has come out of the 90's/early 00's, helped along by teen films such "American Pie". So, get your eyeliner on and pull out your studded belt and checked sweatband. Let's rock out with our socks out!

POP PUNK PLAYLIST

1. BUDDY HOLLY - WEEZER - 1994
2. SELL OUT - REEL BIG FISH - 1996
3. FLAGPOLE SITTA - HARVEY DANGER - 1997
4. JUMPER - THIRD EYE BLIND - 1997
5. SEMI-CHARMED LIFE - THIRD EYE BLIND - 1997
6. WALKING ON THE SUN - SMASHMOUTH - 1997
7. ALL STAR - SMASHMOUTH - 1999
8. OWN WORST ENEMY - LIT - 1999
9. THE MOVIES - ALIEN ANT FARM - 1999
10. DARE YOU TO MOVE - SWITCHFOOT - 2000
11. TEENAGE DIRTBAG - WHEATUS - 2000
12. AMERICAN PSYCHO - TREBLE CHARGER - 2001
13. FLAVOUR OF THE WEEK - AMERICAN HI-FI - 2001
14. PHOEBE CATES - FENIX TX - 2001
15. SMOOTH CRIMINAL - ALIEN ANT FARM - 2001
16. STUPID KID - ALKALINE TRIO - 2001
17. THE MIDDLE - JIMMY EAT WORLD - 2001
18. GET OVER IT - OK GO - 2002
19. GIRL ALL THE BAD GUYS WANT - BOWLING FOR SOUP - 2002
20. MY FRIENDS OVER YOU - NEW FOUND GLORY - 2002
21. PUNK ROCK PRINCESS - SOMETHING CORPORATE - 2002
22. BOYS OF SUMMER - THE ATARIS - 2003
23. OCEAN AVENUE - YELLOWCARD - 2003
24. ONLY ONE - YELLOWCARD - 2003
25. STACY'S MOM - FOUNTAINS OF WAYNE - 2003
26. THE REASON - HOOBASTANK - 2003

POSTMAN PAT. These days you will find Pat delivering special packages via air travel! You would never have seen this in the

90's! Pat was keeping it real with a mere postal van and black and white cat pal, Jess. This simple life was still a struggle for Pat, as he used to mix up the parcels and he would never just have a straightforward shift. Adorable children's show, one of the best.

POWER RANGERS. Live action TV series about five teenagers who call on ancient powers to defend the earth from evil. The ultimate squad goal in all of history. There was a time when we ate, slept and breathed Power Rangers.

PRACTISING THE NIKE TICK. If you went to school in the 90's, look back at all your exercise books and all you will see are terrible variations of the Nike tick. Many kids spent many lessons trying to perfect the tick, some even had it shaved in their hair. Consistency was a big issue, if you got it right once it didn't mean you would get it right again. You may also find several variations of this image.

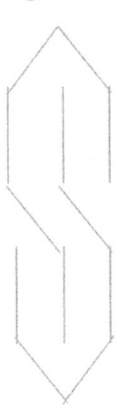

PRETTY WOMAN. Probably still Julia Roberts's most famous role. A laugh out loud rom-com with an iconic end. A story about a businessman and his weekend with a prostitute that takes an unexpected turn. That scene when she goes back to the shop, with that worker that treated here like rubbish is the just the best.

PRINCE OF EGYPT. Animated, musical film by Dreamworks. This film is one of the best non-Disney animations. The soundtrack was so good, even if you weren't religious and didn't speak Hebrew, you still vibed hard to these songs. Then there was the star-studded cast that did the voices. Hey, how does Moses make his coffee? Hebrews it!

PRINCESS DIANA (1961-1997). You can't talk about the 90's without mentioning an actual British treasure, Princess Diana. An English rose. She was beautiful inside and out and her contributions to causes worldwide will always be remembered. Elton said it best in his 1997 "Candle in the Wind" re-make in her honor. The nation will never be out of mourning.

PRODIGY, THE. Exceptional rave band with iconic music vids and headbangin' tunes. Keith Flint had the ultimate electro punk vibe going on. Check out "No Good", "Charly", "Everybody in the Place", "Out of Space", "One Love", "Firestarter", "Breathe" and "Smack My Bitch Up".

PUNK'D. Hidden camera prank show on MTV hosted by Ashton Kutcher. Ashton would prank innocent celebrities on a grand scale. I'm surprised that guy had any friends. There was the IRS taking all of Justin Timberlake's possessions, even his dog. There was Beyonce thinking she ruined Christmas for orphaned kids. It was so cruel and sometimes the pranks really backfired.

PURPLE RONNIE. A stickman cartoon created by Giles Andreae, along with funny poems and doodles. Purple Ronnie has featured in many books, greetings cards and randomly chocolate bars as well.

PUSH POPS. Lollies from the 90's that were in every corner shop in Britain. We loved the novelty of sliding the lolly out of its container. It didn't take a lot, did it!

Q.

QUEEN LATIFAH. Queen Latifah still looks as youthful and fresh-faced as she did in the 90's and we are all very jealous. She's dabbled in singing, rapping and acting. Multi-talented and often described as a feminist rapper. Big hits included "Ladies First", "U.N.I.T.Y" and "Bananas". She starred in the sitcom "Living Single" and in several movies including "Chicago", "Bringing Down the House" and "Scary Movie 3".

QUEEN'S NOSE, THE. A TV series adapted from the books by Dick King-Smith about a girl who has a magical coin that makes her wildest dreams come true. We spent our time rubbing 50ps in hopes the same magic would happen to us.

R.

R&B. 90's R&B was amazing, R&B music in its prime! are some one-off hits that will bring back memories of parties, school days and general life back then. You are welcome.

R&B AND REGGAE CLASSICS

1. I WANNA SEX YOU UP - COLOR ME BADD - 1991
2. SWEAT - INNER CIRCLE - 1992
3. TWO CAN PLAY THAT GAME - BOBBY BROWN - 1992
4. BUMP N GRIND - R.KELLY - 1993
5. NO NO NO - DAWN PENN - 1994
6. FREAK LIKE ME - ADINA HOWARD - 1995
7. SHY GUY - DIANA KING - 1995
8. THA CROSSROADS - BONES, THUGS N HARMONY - 1995
9. THIS IS HOW WE DO IT - MONTELL JORDAN - 1995
10. PONY - GINUWINE - 1996
11. RETURN OF THE MACK - MARK MORRISON - 1996
12. BOY IS MINE - BRANDY & MONICA - 1998
13. HEADS HIGH - MR VEGAS - 1998
14. ALWAYS COME BACK TO YOUR LOVE - SAMANTHA MUMBA - 2000
15. CASE OF THE EX - MYA - 2000
16. SHACKLES - MARY MARY - 2000
17. ALL FOR YOU - JANET JACKSON - 2001
18. AM TO PM - CHRISTINA MILIAN - 2001
19. ANOTHER DAY IN PARADISE - BRANDY & RAY J - 2002
20. NO LETTING GO - WAYNE WONDER - 2002
21. TURN ME ON - KEVIN LYTTLE - 2002
22. IGNITION REMIX - R.KELLY - 2003
23. NO DIGGITY - BLACKSTREET - 2003
24. REAL THINGS - JAVINE - 2003
25. DUDE - BEENIE MAN - 2004

RAP. My next amazing playlist for you lovely people is rap. We had some wicked rap songs back then. Here are some hits to add to your 90's/00's mash-up.

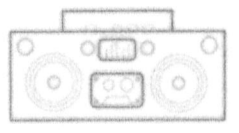

BIGGEST RAP HITS

1. I WANNA GIVE YOU (DEVOTION) - NOMAD - 1991
2. NOW THAT WE'VE FOUND LOVE - HEAVY D & THE BOYZ - 1991
3. BABY GOT BACK - SIR MIX-A-LOT - 1992
4. BOOM BOOM BOOM - THE OUTHERE BROTHERS - 1992
5. INFORMER - SNOW - 1992
6. JUMP AROUND - HOUSE OF PAIN - 1992
7. COME BABY COME - K7 - 1993
8. WHOOMP THERE IT IS - TAG TEAM - 1993
9. DON'T STOP (WIGGLE WIGGLE) - THE OUTHERE BROTHERS - 1994
10. HERE COMES THE HOTSTEPPER - INI KAMOZE - 1994
11. GANGSTERS PARADISE - COOLIO - 1995
12. I GOT 5 ON IT - LUNIZ - 1995
13. C U WHEN U GET THERE - COOLIO FT 40 THEVZ - 1997
14. FEEL SO GOOD - MASE - 1997
15. GONE TIL NOVEMBER - WYCLEF JEAN - 1997
16. IT'S LIKE THAT - RUN DMC FT JASON NEVINS - 1997
17. TURN IT UP - BUSTA RHYMES - 1997
18. WHO AM I - BEENIE MAN - 1997
19. GHETTO SUPERSTAR - PRAS - 1998
20. FREESTYLER - BOMFUNK MC'S - 1999
21. GOT YOUR MONEY - OL DIRTY BASTARD - 1999
22. JUMP - KRISS KROSS - 1999
23. WHAT WOULD YOU DO - CITY HIGH - 1999
24. COLD AS ICE - M.O.P - 2000
25. PERFECT GENTLEMAN - WYCLEF JEAN - 2000
26. LET ME BLOW YA MIND - EVE FT GWEN STEFANI - 2001
27. MOVE GET OUT THE WAY - LUDACRIS - 2001
28. PURPLE HILLS - D12 - 2001
29. WHO'S THAT GIRL - EVE - 2001
30. WITNESS THE FITNESS - ROOTS MANUVA - 2001

RAP METAL. Genre of music that combines hip hop and rock, started in the 80's but hit major popularity in the 90's. Here are some songs to break stuff too.

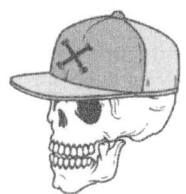

RAP METAL PLAYLIST

1. KILLING IN THE NAME OF - RAGE AGAINST THE MACHINE - 1991
2. FREAK ON A LEASH - KORN - 1998
3. PRETTY FLY FOR A WHITE GUY - THE OFFSPRING - 1998
4. WHY DONT YOU GET A JOB? - THE OFFSPRING - 1998
5. BREAK STUFF - LIMP BIZKIT - 1999
6. BUTTERFLY - CRAZYTOWN - 1999
7. CRAWLING - LINKIN PARK - 2000
8. HEAVEN IS A HALFPIPE - OPM - 2000
9. LAST RESORT - PAPA ROACH - 2000
10. MY WAY - LIMP BIZKIT - 2000
11. ROLLIN - LIMP BIZKIT - 2000
12. WANT YOU BAD - THE OFFSPRING - 2000
13. BETWEEN ANGELS AND INSECTS - PAPA ROACH - 2001
14. IN THE END - LINKIN PARK - 2002
15. STARRY EYED SUPRISE - PAUL OAKENFOLD - 2002
16. BRING ME TO LIFE - EVANESCENCE - 2003
17. FAINT - LINKIN PARK - 2003
18. NUMB - LINKIN PARK - 2003

RAVE MUSIC. Genre of music that is a variation of house/techno/electro and dance. Get your neon on, decorate your room in glow sticks and get your rave on with "Ebeneezer Goode" by The Shamen, "On a Ragga Trip" by SL2, "Insomnia" by Faithless, "Born Slippy" by Underworld and "Set You Free" by N-Trance.

RAVEN. I'm still waiting for the cloak to become a fashion statement. This show took six kids, dressed them up in coloured medieval sacks and made them work together to fight a villain. Don't worry it was a gameshow and didn't put kids in actual danger. The Raven himself used to shout out cryptic messages like "the eye of the raven is with you". Yes, thank you Raven, so helpful.

RAYMAN. A franchise of platform video games released in 1995 with games over various platforms. "Raving Rabbids" was a spinoff of the original Rayman series. "Rayman Legends" deserves an exhibition in an art gallery, it is visually stunning.

R.E.M. I want the eternal youth serum that lead singer, Michael Stipe, has taken. That dude hasn't changed since the 80's. "Losing My Religion" was one of the most 90's hits of the 90's. They also did a powerful ballad "Everybody Hurts" and the polar opposite "Shiny Happy People", Other big songs for them in this era were "Man on the Moon" and "Imitation of Life".

READY, STEADY, COOK! Daytime cooking show originally hosted by Fern Brittan but then taken over by Ainsley Harriott in 2000. Two teams competed to make the best 3-course meal. Total food heaven.

REDGRAVE, STEVE. Our homegrown Olympic legend, Sir Steve Redgrave. The only rower EVER to have won FIVE gold medals. CONSECUTIVELY. From 1984 to 2000 Redgrave was smashin the rowing game and is arguably Britain's best Olympian ever, ever. He was knighted in 2001. You go Sir Redgrave.

RED HOT CHILLI PEPPERS. Red Hot Chilli Peppers, in all their shirtless glory really made it big in the 90's. Rock band who are incredibly good to see live. If you listened to any Alternative radio back then, you would definitely know all their main bangers. "Blood Sugar Sex Magik", "Californication" and "By the Way" are albums you must hear before you die.

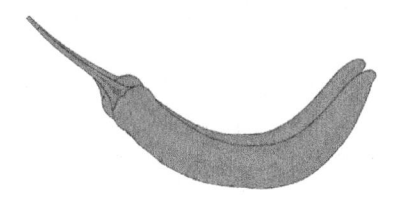

REEVES, KEANU. So many people say that Keanu Reeves is the best action movie actor of all time. He was also a heart throb and back in the day. Remember, he is also very funny, especially in "Bill and Ted", of which the sequel came out in the 90's. Other big movies of Keanu's were "Point Break", "Speed", "The Matrix Trilogy", "Bram Stoker's Dracula", "The Devil's Advocate" and "My Own Private Idaho".

REN AND STIMPY. Animated TV series following a mentally unstable chihuahua and a cat with one sandwich short of a picnic. Recipe for disaster? Correct.

RENNISON, LOUISE. The author of the "Angus, Thongs and Full-Frontal Snogging" book series! Fire up the group chat ladies, what girl didn't read these in her early teens!? Georgia Nicolson was hilarious and unfortunately for us, relatable.

RICCI, CHRISTINA. Actress who made Wednesday Addams and the girl from "Casper" come to life. Because of this she will always be acting royalty to me. She lent her voice to "Small Soldiers" as well. Of course, Tim Burton would snap her up for "Sleepy Hollow" and she did an amazing portrayal of Selby Wall in "Monster" with Charlize Theron.

RICHIE RICH. Richie Rich was originally a comic in the 50's but I'm talking about the 1994 film starring Macauley Culkin. This film was literally every kid's dreams come true. Imagine the adventures you could have around that estate. AND HE HAD A MCDONALDS. Let's play tag, ON QUAD BIKES. Importantly the movie did show us that even with all that dollar and status, true friendship and teamwork will always be the most important.

RICHIE, GUY. Director of some crackin' British films. If you don't fall in love with the cockney-ness then we can't be friends. "Lock, Stock and Two Smoking Barrels" and "Snatch" were his first two movies and remain his best. Hilarious script, gritty and great acting by all.

RICKI LAKE SHOW, THE. One of the chat shows that came out of the chat show boom that hit the 90's. Ricki discussed current issues with guests and her audience and occasionally went a bit deeper into more serious issues. "Mom Let Me Do It In The House Or I'm Gone", "I'm Gay, But Today I Want To Try Going The Other Way", "You Think Your Naked Bod Is the Bomb, but Your Internet Pics Are Nasty.Com". All authentic Ricki Lake episode titles, That's why it was one of the best shows on TV.

RIMES, LEANN. When you think of women in country music LeAnn is on everyone's list. She was like a 90's Taylor Swift. She took us on an emotional ride with "How Do I Live", she rocked those cowboy boots and got down and dirty in "Can't Fight the Moonlight". "I Need You" and "Life Goes On", also tunes.

ROBOT WARS. The original "Robot Wars" series broadcast from 1998 to 2004. Some of those robots on that show will 100% rise up and take over all of humankind. I'm sorry but some of them were mental. This show is where two teams build their own robot and battle it out against another robot, whichever robot crushes the other is the winner. When the robots do take over the world they will make humans fight to the death, like old school Gladiators (Romans not the TV Show). And they will see us as a bloodthirsty sport. The horror…... But how good was Craig Charles though!?

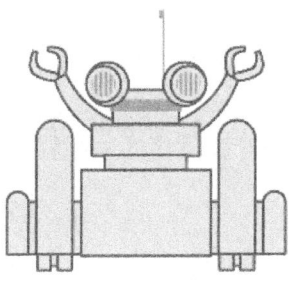

ROCKET POWER. Rocket Power might have been a lesser known Nickelodeon cartoon to some. It followed a group of four young friends who all shared a passion for extreme sports. Every parent's dream. It taught us to stick by our friends even in moments of failure and risk.

ROCK MUSIC. Remember these used to be our anthems! When any of these songs become "classic rock" you may as well reserve me the next room in a retirement home. Some killer air guitar moments here, made slightly more real by the release of Guitar Hero in the mid-00's. Enjoy!

AIR GUITAR MOMENTS

1. UNBELIEVABLE - EMF - 1990
2. WALKING IN MEMPHIS - MARC COHN - 1991
3. CREEP - RADIOHEAD - 1993
4. ZOMBIE - THE CRANBERRIES - 1993
5. FLY AWAY - LENNY KRAVITZ - 1998
6. IRIS - GOO GOO DOLLS - 1998
7. AMAZED - LONESTAR - 1999
8. HATE TO SAY I TOLD YOU SO - THE HIVES - 2000
9. ALIVE - P.O.D - 2001
10. CHOP SUEY - SYSTEM OF A DOWN - 2001
11. HOW YOU REMIND ME - NICKELBACK - 2001
12. IT'S BEEN AWHILE - STAIND - 2001
13. LEFT BEHIND - SLIPKNOT - 2001
14. PARTY HARD - ANDREW WK - 2001
15. PLUG IN BABY - MUSE - 2001
16. SHE HATES ME - PUDDLE OF MUDD - 2001
17. ALWAYS - SALIVA - 2002
18. HATE EVERYTHING ABOUT YOU - THREE DAYS GRACE - 2003
19. IN THE SHADOWS - THE RASMUS - 2003
20. TIME IS RUNNING OUT - MUSE - 2003

ROCKO'S MODERN LIFE. Surreal, animated TV show about a wallaby named Rocko. Did we think an eccentric wallaby moving to the USA was going to be a good idea? This poor guy can't cope with the weight of modern life. He's surrounded by annoying neighbours and advantage taking pals, he just needs a break! You can see why people found it relatable for a cartoon and it bagged itself a Daytime Emmy award.

ROGERS, GINGER (1911-1995). Actress, singer and incredible dancer best remembered for her on-screen pairings with Fred Astaire. She was joined by Fred Astaire in a total of 10 movies. Fun fact! Her actual name was Virginia but her cousin couldn't pronounce it, so Ginger was born. A sad loss for the world of film, dance and the rest.

ROLIE POLIE OLIE. French-Canadian, animated, children's show about a clockwork boy living in a robotic world. The buildings in the neighbourhood all had faces. That was oddly satisfying.

ROSIE AND JIM. Classic children's TV show. Author, John Cunliffe, used his puppets, Rosie and Jim, to tell stories and go on educational adventures. Are Rosie and Jim brother and sister? Are they dating? It annoys me that John doesn't clear this up. This show is one of those that make me realise we really were living our best life in the 90's. Oh and John Cunliffe also created "Postman Pat", what a ledge.

ROTTEN RALPH. Stop motion animation about a mean and mischievous cat who is always playing practical jokes on his owners. No idea why they put up with Ralph's s**t. This guy could have made David Attenborough cry.

ROUND THE TWIST. Australian fantasy TV show about a family who live in a lighthouse and have many magical adventures. This show was based on a book by Australian children's author, Paul Jennings. Most kids will remember seeing his books in the school library, with titles such as "Undone", "Unmentionable" and "Quirky Tales". His stories were always strange, very out there and like no other.

ROWNTREES BUGS. If these ever make it back on the shelves I will lift them in the air like a new-born Simba. They were jelly bugs with a liquid centre that burst in your mouth when bitten into. The gooey, oozy, fruity liquid was like the nectar of the gods. Come on Rowntrees, bring them back!

ROYLE FAMILY, THE. A TV series centred around a family from Manchester who sit around and watch TV, I genuinely thought this show was about the actual Royal Family, as in the monarchy, just watching TV. I was very wrong. This show is great to binge watch, think "Shameless" without the sex.

RUGBY WORLD CUP 2003. Jonny Wilkinson was Britain's drop kick hero that year, with THAT match winning moment. Him and Jason Robinson really helped to open rugby up to a wider audience. In 2003 WE, yes that's us, ENGLAND, won the World Cup. We beat Australia in Australia!! I know, it's unbelievable but it happened!

RUGRATS. Children's TV show on Nickelodeon following the adventures of Tommy Pickles, Chucky, Phil, Lil and Angelica. Also, the only tune you could play on the keyboard. Feature films came from the series and other characters such as Dil and Kimmy were introduced later on. A series called "All Grown Up" was created about when the babies were in school and no longer babies. Remember I said I love a fan theory, well there's a theory that the babies aren't real, and they are fragments of Angelica's mind, made up as a way to cope with her absent parents. Interesting. Fun fact, the lady who voiced Bart Simpson, Nancy Cartwright, also did the voice for Chucky!

RUSH HOUR. Hilarious movie franchise starring Jackie Chan and Chris Tucker. Chris Tucker and Jackie Chan's frenemy relationship is too funny. Jackie amazingly does his own stunts and there are some serious moves that go down in these movies. Very impressive and Chris Tucker cracks me up.

RYAN, MEG. Meg Ryan starred in some fab movies during the 80's and even more fab movies in the 90's. Her and Tom Hanks made the best rom-com couple. She has now vanished off the planet and this is so sad. 90's/00's movies of hers include "Sleepless in Seattle", "French Kiss", "Anastasia", "City of Angels" and "You've Got Mail".

RYDER, WINONA. Ultimate 90's actress and babe. Winona Ryder starred in many movies, working on several occasions with Tim Burton. She was also famously dating Johnny Depp at the time and the two of them were the ultimate couple goal. Her best movies during this era were "Edward Scissorhands", "Night on Earth" and "Girl Interrupted".

S.

SABRINA THE TEENAGE WITCH. Nickelodeon TV series starring Melissa Joan Hart as a high school teenager with witchy powers. Who didn't want to be a part of the Spellman clan? Who didn't want a sassy, talking cat like Salem? There was also a magazine that came out, "Sabrina Secrets" and it came with a free purple sparkly jewellery box with free jewellery with each issue. Melissa was also in another hit TV show "Clarissa Explains All", a show filled with fashion moments. That girl was not afraid to mix patterns.

SAMPRAS, PETE. American tennis player who won 14 grand slam titles, which was a record at the time but has since been beaten. A whopping 7 of these wins were Wimbledon wins. He is often considered the best tennis player of all time.

SANDLER, ADAM. Zany and wacky comedian who seems to be marmite with people. There is the crazy, stupid type comedy of "Billy Madison", "Waterboy" and "Little Nicky". But his best movies are where he has toned it down a bit and there's a bit more heart. Top movies during this era were "Happy Gilmore", "The Wedding Singer", "Big Daddy", "Mr Deeds" and "Anger Management".

SAVAGE GARDEN. The band that had us all slow dancing with our middle school sweetheart. So romantic. When I hear their songs it just takes me back to a simpler time. Best hits were "I

Knew I Loved You", "To the Moon and Back" and "Truly Madly Deeply".

SAVED BY THE BELL. Our favourite high school teens who were everyone's crushes. I think even the guys had a man crush on Zack as well as Kelly. How fashion was this show!? A treasure trove of statement making and the ultimate 90's wardrobe. The garish, graphic jumpers and shirts! Those shirts and huge phones meant privacy was way off the cards. Probably the best high school comedy/drama of the decade.

SCARY MOVIE. Scary Movie 1, 2 and 3 came out way back during 2000-2003. For those that are unfamiliar, Scary Movie is a series of movies that parody and take the mick out of horror movies. The first movie is a parody of "Scream". The second movie is set in a haunted house. Shawn and Marlon Wayans star as the main characters along with Anna Faris and Regina Hall. Truly the Wayans brothers' best work.

SCHOOL DAYS. I miss being at school complaining about being at school. So many memories of school during the 90's/00's. The playground games, "What's the Time Mr Wolf?",

"Grandma's Footsteps", "Red Rover", "British Bulldog" and "Stuck in the Mud". The flimsy black plimsolls you had to wear with the elasticated front. Kids of today won't know the struggles of choosing what Word Art to use on their homework. Microsoft Word won't ever use that little paperclip guy to give us hints and tips again. If you went to school during this era, how many of the following do you remember?

SCHOOL DAYS

- *FEELING LIKE A KING SITTING ON THE BENCHES IN ASSEMBLY, WHILST THE MINIONS WERE ON THE HALL FLOOR. HOPEFULLY YOU DIDN'T HAVE TO SIT ON THE KNOBBLY BIT THOUGH BECAUSE THAT WAS A PAIN LIKE NO OTHER.*

- *GIGGLING AT THE LAME JOKES IN YOUR CGP REVISION BOOKS.*

- *THE MULTICOLOURED CUBES THAT JOINED TOGETHER TO HELP YOU LEARN MATH. ALSO DOING YOUR MATH HOMEWORK ON THE "MY MATHS" WEBSITE.*

- *PRETENDING TO SHARPEN YOUR PENCIL AT THE BIN BUT REALLY IT WAS A STRATEGICALLY PLANNED CHAT WITH YOUR FRIEND. THE EQUIVALENT OF AN OFFICE FAG BREAK.*

- PEELING PVA GLUE OFF YOUR HANDS.

- THE FIRST, FRESH PAGE OF A NEW EXERCISE BOOK AND THEN TAKING IT HOME TO BACK IT WITH WRAPPING PAPER OR OLD WALLPAPER.

- BEING PICKED ON TO HAND THE WHITEBOARDS OUT AND GIVING THE PERSON YOU'RE NOT TALKING TO THE DIRTY ONE.

- FEELING LIKE A PACK HORSE WHEN YOU HAD PE AND FOOD TECH ON THE SAME DAY. PRAYING YOU WOULDN'T FALL OVER BECAUSE THERE WAS NO GETTING UP.

- THE RUSH OF EXCITEMENT THAT WENT ROUND THE ASSEMBLY HALL LIKE A MEXICAN WAVE WHEN THE ANNOUNCEMENT WAS MADE THAT THE FIELD WAS OPEN FOR SUMMER.

- THE RUMOR THAT INK ERASERS WERE MADE OUT OF PIG'S WEE.

- BEROL HANDWRITING PENS

- CHRISTMAS AT PRIMARY SCHOOL DOING FUN SHIZZ, FEELING LIKE A DON BRINGING IN YOUR COCKTAIL SAUSAGES FOR THE BUFFET, BRINGING IN GAMES LIKE "SCREWBALL SCRAMBLE" TO PLAY AND THEN THE CHRISTMAS MOVIE ON THE WHEEL OUT TV.

- **REBEL CHILDREN TRYING TO BLIND THE TEACHER USING THEIR WATCH OR RULER AND THE REFLECTION OF THE SUN.**

- **THOSE FOOTBALLS THAT HAD THE LEATHER PEELING OFF THEM. WHEN IT RAINED THEY BECAME SO HEAVY AND FULL ON SMACKED SOMEONE IN THE FACE, YOU COULD HEAR THE STING FOLLOWED BY "OOOOOOOO".**

- **THE "AQA ANTHOLOGY" THAT RUINED YOUR ENGLISH LIFE. IF I EVER SEE A TED HUGHES POEM AGAIN *SHAKES FIST*.**

- **LIP SYNC BATTLE WAS CREATED WAY BACK IN PRIMARY SCHOOL, MOUTHING THE WORDS TO HYMNS. "SING HOSANNAH TO THE KING OF KINGS."**

- **WHY WHEN IT WAS YOUR BIRTHDAY DID YOU GIVE SWEETS TO EVERYONE? SHOULDN'T YOU BE GETTING THE SWEETS.**

- **LAUGHING AT THE KID THAT ACCIDENTALLY CALLED THE TEACHER "MUM".**

SCHOOL DINNERS. Oh the good old days of school dinners. You can't beat a good plate of processed meat and veg after a PE sesh, especially if it was gymnastics that day (seriously those mats stung harder than if you just hit the floor). Do you remember these school dinner heroes?

SCHOOL DINNER STAPLES

1. CORNFLAKE TART
2. CARAMEL TART
3. PINK CUSTARD
4. VANILLA SPONGE WITH ICING AND SPRINKLES
5. CHOCOLATE TOOTHPASTE
6. RICE PUDDING WITH A BLOB OF JAM
7. TURKEY DINOSAURS
8. SMILEY POTATO FACES
9. TURKEY TWIZZLERS
10. SPOTTED DICK
11. JAM ROLY POLY

SCHWARZENEGGER, ARNOLD. The 90's was a fab era for Arnold's movie career. He kicked it off with "Total Recall", then onto comedy "Kindergarten Cop" and THEN the sequel to "The Terminator". Next, "Last Action Hero", "True Lies" and then he moved onto bonkers comedy "Junior", yes Arnold plays a pregnant man. Please don't ask, it's not as bad as it sounds. Christmas comedy caper "Jingle All The Way" was so bad it's good. In 2003 a third "Terminator" came out. We won't go into "Batman and Robin", we'll bypass that one. Hey, Arnold! We love ya!

S CLUB 7. Successful mixed band of the 90's/00's containing who went on to have their own TV series and even a junior version of their band, "S Club Juniors". Pump any S Club tune at a birthday party and kids would go crazy for it, jumping and drawing "S"'s in the air. There really was no party like an S Club party! When the band split the only one to really do anything solo was Rachel Stevens who released a steamy vid to go with "L.A Ex". Later she released "More More More" and "Some Girls".

S CLUB 7 & THE JUNIORS

1. BRING IT ALL BACK - 1999
2. S CLUB PARTY - 1999
3. TWO IN A MILLION - 1999
4. YOU'RE MY NO.1 - 1999
5. REACH - 2000
6. NATURAL - 2000
7. NEVER HAD A DREAM COME TRUE - 2000
8. DON'T STOP MOVIN - 2001
9. HAVE YOU EVER - 2001
10. YOU - 2002
11. ONE STEP CLOSER - S CLUB JUNIORS - 2002
12. AUTOMATIC HIGH - S CLUB JUNIORS - 2002
13. NEW DIRECTION - S CLUB JUNIORS - 2002
14. PUPPY LOVE - S CLUB JUNIORS - 2002

SEAL. R&B and ballad singer, famously married to Heidi Klum at one stage. His biggest hit was "Kiss From a Rose" but also had an awesome hit with "Crazy" and with dance act Adamski, "Killer".

SECRET GARDEN, THE. Originally a book but turned into a film in 1993. A young British girl is orphaned due to a disaster in India, where she was living. Because of this she is sent to live in her uncle's castle where she soon discovers the garden and its many secrets. I spent many afternoons roaming around my nan's garden hoping I would fall on some secret area. Sadly it never happened.

SCRUNCHIES. Every girl had a scrunchie in their hair in the 90's. Whether it was tight, high ponytail that you forced your poor mum to do over and over until there were no bumps and it was perfectly smooth. Or channeling Deb from "Napoleon Dynamite" and going for a side pony. Watch this space velvet scrunchie, you'll be coming back out the closet in no time.

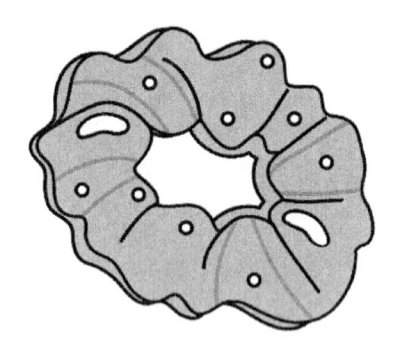

SCORSESE, MARTIN. This amazing director brought out several HUGE movies during this period. Most notably "Goodfellas", "Cape Fear", "Casino" and "Gangs of New York". Joe Pesci in "Goodfellas" is terrifyingly good and Robert De Niro is terrifying in "Cape Fear". Sideshow Bob, also terrifying in this role.

SEGA CONSOLES. SEGA released several consoles over this period but the most popular was the Megadrive, which came out in 1990 and the Dreamcast released in 1999. There were so many Megadrive memories that Nintendo kids missed out on. The special stage on "Sonic 2", knocking your friends off their motorbike into sheep on "Road Rash", dancing as MJ in "Moonwalker", just too many to mention.

SELECTION STOCKINGS AT CHRISTMAS. Us Brits can never believe it when it's nearly Christmas. Next to the weather, it's our favourite thing to talk about. "Can you believe it's September already, 3 months to Christmas!". One blast from the past, the selection stocking! You know, the ones that were like netting with chocolate bars inside. Where have they gone!? Also selection boxes, 100% shrunk in size, they used to be MEGA. AND does anyone else remember the advent calendars that went up to New Years Day!! I swear I'm not making them up. Every 5 minutes on Christmas day you're like "what could be more important than having a little something to eat" and the selection stocking was perfect to fill those needs in between dinners.

SEQUINS. Sequins and glitter were da bomb, sequin dresses, sequin tops, we couldn't resist the glam! There were the jeans with a sequin union jack in the pocket area and the jeans that felt kind of slippery and sparkled. We also loved diamantes on jean back pockets. Talking of diamantes, the "Playboy" and "Von Dutch" baseball caps. Chav-chic.

SEX AND THE CITY. Super popular rom-com, drama series. The four main ladies were Carrie, Samantha, Miranda and Charlotte. We watched this and thought #friendshipgoals but then watching it as adults we quickly realised their relationship was pretty toxic! Carrie especially used to make some really poor life choices. Actually all of them were kind of terrible role models, but what can you do, we loved the show anyway!

SHAGGY. Jamaican reggae and rap singer whose famous songs include "It Wasn't Me", "Mr Boombastic", "Angel" and "Oh Carolina". Does Shaggy even rap actual words?

SHAKESPEARE. Shakespeare was slaying from beyond the grave it in the 90's! There were some wicked movie adaptations of his plays, some designed more for teenagers so they kind of got twisted into teen comedies. "The Lion King" was actually inspired by "Hamlet" but wasn't technically an adaptation. Kenneth Branagh the KING of Shakespeare was fab in "Othello", "Hamlet" and "Much Ado About Nothing". Julia Styles starred in two teen adaptations, "O" based on "Othello" and "10 Things I Hate About You" based on "The Taming of the Shrew". Baz Luhrmann modernised "Romeo and Juliet" with Leonardo DiCaprio, Claire Danes and that bangin Cardigans hit. Kirsten Dunst and Ben Foster also starred in "Get Over It" which was loosely based on "A Midsummer Nights Dream". Isn't it great we are still celebrating Shakespeare's work after all these years. I know we hated him for ruining every English lesson ever but give a brother some credit, he was one mean storyteller.

SHAKIRA. Columbian beauty with a very distinctive, deep singing voice. Her main hits in the early 00's were "Whenever Wherever" and "Underneath Your Clothes".

SHOCKWAVE GAMES. Kings of the online gaming world. So many games we loved in the 90's/00's. They also showed webisodes like "Radiskull and Devil Doll". Some of the best games included "Water Balloon 3". "Donut Boy" and "Fat Boy Raids the Cookie Factory".

SHOOTING STARS. Surreal comedy panel show hosted by Vic Reeves and Bob Mortimer. That description made more sense than the show ever did. The captains for each team were Ulrika Jonsson and Mark Lamarr. Matt Lucas played scorekeeper, a giant baby called George Dawes. "Eranu", "Uvavu".

SHOUT MAGAZINE. Every girl was mad for a girl mag back then. Technology has totally killed this. Gone are the days of relying on magazines for fashion, goss and life lessons. Loads of future celebs used to grace the cover as cover models, including Holly Willoughby, Emma Willis and Keeley Hawes. Fearne Cotton had a section "Fearne's Favourite Things" and they auto became everyone else's fav things.

SIMCITY. A video game that allowed you to design and run your own city, yesss please! The power trip that comes with creating and running an entire city is deadly, seriously, did any of you ever burn down your city just for LOLZ? This is why no human ever should play god.

SIMPLE LIFE, THE. Another MTV reality show, this time following rich girls Paris Hilton and Nicole Ritchie joining a middle-class family and doing everyday jobs like us average joes. They said goodbye to the limo and LA mansion and hello to a public bus and a checkout. A show that highlighted they had no clue what the real world was actually like.

SIMPLE PLAN. Pop punk band whose songs were great to belt out when you felt sorry for yourself or you weren't getting your way with mum and dad. Best songs were "I'm Just a Kid", "Perfect" and "Welcome to My Life".

SIMPLY RED. Mick Hucknall and his spicy ginger locks. Extremely popular band here in the UK. Big hits included "Fairground", "Stars", "For Your Babies", "Angel", "The Air That I Breathe", "Sunrise" and "You Make Me Feel Brand New".

SIMPSONS, THE. The Simpsons started in the 80's and yes, it is still going, but I am talking 90's Simpsons. The Simpsons is the best cartoon ever made but sadly has now become the greatest cartoon of all time that's gone on for too long. The Simpsons really was at its peak during the 90's/early 00's. There is a classic moment or line in every episode. The Simpsons have predicted the future in many of their episodes too, which is super freaky and watching it back as an adult there are so many jokes that went over my head as a kid. As well as the TV show there were the video games that came out too. Many arcade style and platform games, but the best game was "Virtual Springfield" where you could walk round Springfield and go in the various buildings, Then there was "Road Rage" which was like "Crazy Taxi". Even better though was "Hit and Run" which was like a Simpsons, child friendly "GTA". So much merch was out there from books, comics, clothing, toys, games, CDs. We were all obsessed.

SIMS, THE. Hands down the best and most life-changing game ever. So much graft went into creating the ideal Sim family and house, casually dropping the "motherlode" cheat when times were tough. We had spin offs like "Bustin Out" and "Urbz" but the classic "Sims 1" with all its expansion packs was the one. The whole god complex was a major issue when playing The Sims. We did some sick, messed up stuff. Making a sim have no energy, putting them in the swimming pool and removing the steps so they drowned. Starting a fire in a room and taking away the doors. WHAT ARE WE. The shame when you played as the "Goth" family and Cassandra Goth got sent to military school. So many memories. It is hilarious when you think about it. Video games are designed for you to create your wildest fantasies and escape reality for a while. So why on earth were we all in love with a game where we got a house, a job, met a partner and had kids!?

SINATRA, FRANK (1915-1998). "The King of Swing", "Old Blue Eyes". Frank Sinatra first rose to fame in the 40's singing big band numbers and swing music. From there he progressed into movies where he even won an Oscar as a supporting actor for "From Here to Eternity". He was also part of the rat pack and was famously friends with Humphrey Bogart and Lauren Bacall. He dated a string of famous women at the time. With a voice so smooth, it's impossible to mention all his incredible performances. Biggest movies were "On the Town", "Guys and Dolls"," Oceans 11" and "High Society".

SISTER ACT. Comedy musical and one of Whoopi Goldberg's most famous roles. The first movie came out in 1992 followed by a sequel in 1993. Whoopi plays a singer who witnessed a mob crime, so to protect her the police disguise her as a nun and hide her in a convent. A fun family movie with a great cast. There really is nun better.

SISTER SISTER. Kids of today will not know the rush of holding a wee in until an ad break, sprinting to the loo, waiting for your sibling to start shouting "IT'S ON". We didn't have "pause" in our day kiddies! Sister Sister was a show you didn't want to miss a second of. It was about twins Tia and Tamera who were split at birth and adopted. They chance meet each other later on in life and both families agree to move in together. Totally unrealistic but whatever, it was funny, and it made us wish we had a twin of our own.

SIXTH SENSE, THE. Horror/thriller by director M. Night Shyamalan, starring Bruce Willis and Hayley Joel Osmant. There is a very famous twist and in the slight chance you don't know it I won't ruin it for you. It is a great film and actually worth a re-watch even if you know the twist, as you pick things up you didn't the first time and its fun spotting the clues.

SIZE OF SNACKS. I don't care what anyone says, snacks have decreased in size. Chocolate bars costing 80p each are more like a fun size bar. Why do they call them fun size when they are smaller? I'd have more fun if the bar was bigger, wouldn't you? Women who say their wedding day is the best day of their life haven't experienced two snacks falling out of a vending machine by mistake. Just saying, a "Snickers" in the 90's weighed 60g, today a mere 48g. Don't get me started on crisps. There are about 6 crisps in one packet. Everyone can relate to the rage when you think you have one left, and it turns out they're all gone. Bring back the original sizes!

SKATER FASHION. Baggy jeans for boys with a chain wallet attached, chunky trainers like "Vans", "Converse" or "DC" and a backwards cap or beanie. We also loved the graphic t-shirt over a long sleeve top look too. Girls also liked a baggy jean but also a ripped jean. The baggy jean was a nightmare when it was raining out, half your leg would get soaked. I'd say about 20% of us could actually skateboard, the rest of us were just in it for Tony Hawks and rock music.

SKIP IT. Addictive toy that kept kids active and off the sofa. It took a bit of coordination, you put one foot through a loop and swung it round your ankle. At the other end there was a ball, and you would have to jump over it. If you took it into the playground and you fell over it was fine because the dinner ladies would be ready with a wet paper towel. As any British school child will know, a wet paper towel can solve anything from a mild concussion to a broken leg. Many casualties were caused by "Skip It".

SKIRTS OVER TROUSERS. Yes, it was a look and it wasn't a put together look, oh no, you brought a skirt already attached to a trouser, so a skrouser I guess. You could purchase these from "Tammy Girl" and bust them out on mufti day. Some looks have to be left in the 90's and I am praying that's where it'll stay.

SKY DANCERS. Line of toys that spun their wings and flew into the air. When you set one off you knew you needed to get the hell out of the way because if they landed on you, they hurt like somethin' else.

SLAP BRACELETS. The satisfying feeling of slapping these on your wrist and the feeling of it curling round your arm. BUT if the fabric had torn and the exposed metal was poking out, it would feel like your arm skin had just been ripped off.

SLEEPOVER CLUB, THE. Book series that later became a TV series. The Australians did a great job of casting girls that actually looked like the girls on the front cover of the books. The show followed various adventures they had. I remember watching this at breakfast time and often having the subtitles on because I'd be crunching too loud on my cereal.

SLIDE PHONES. When flip phones moved aside, the slide phone came to take its place. I think we should go back to having messaging systems that don't show you when people are typing, it would alleviate the anger when someone is typing for ages and you are waiting for this epic speech and all you get is an "ok". We were well grown up having a slide phone with a full-on mini keyboard. Not as dramatic as slamming a flip phone but a forceful slide up still felt satisfying.

SLIP DRESSES. Worn over a white t-shirt for bonus 90's points. You could have an evening slip dress in a sexual silk or satin, or even velvet. You could play it casual with a floral or denim looking one. Super versatile with those beautiful, feminine spaghetti straps to show off your collarbone and shoulders.

SMACK THE PONY. All-female comedy sketch show. This was a great show, especially for women, as it was one of the first comedies that made light of everyday female issues.

SMALL SOLDIERS. American sci-fi, part animated, part live action movie. This movie is about a teenager getting some soldier action figures, however these figures and their enemies have had a microchip installed by their creators, intended for them to wage war on each other. Toys and even humans are tortured! A kid friendly movie about a science experiment gone wrong, but should be taken a lot more seriously than it is.

SMART! Children's art show, home of the famous clay man "Morph", shown on CBBC. They used to turn everyday objects into arty pieces, similar to "Art Attack".

SMASH HITS MAGAZINE. Music magazine that often came with free CD's or posters for your bedroom wall. Who doesn't love a tell-all interview!? Of course we needed to know how in love Britney and Justin were. It was crucial that we knew the secret lives of Atomic Kitten. We relied on this magazine to keep us in the loop with it all.

SMITH, WILL. Rapper and actor who blasted onto the scene in the 90's. He had major success with "Fresh Prince of Bel Air" and began his rap career as the fresh prince with DJ Jazzy Jeff. Biggest successes were "Summertime", "The Fresh Prince Rap" and "Boom Shake the Room". After getting off the Fresh Prince train, Will released some rap hits, some for the films he was in like "Men in Black", "Wild Wild West" and "Black Suits Comin". Then he had hits with "Gettin Jiggy With It", "Miami", "Just the Two of Us" and "Will 2K". His film career really took off too, with fab buddy cop film "Bad Boys" and the sequel, end of the world epic "Independence Day", family favourite "Men in Black" and the sequel. He also did an incredible portrayal of Muhammad Ali in "Ali". What a talent!

SOAP MOMENTS. Us Brits love our soaps. The 90's/early 00's saw so many jaw dropping moments. We were excited about Eastenders, cuckoo about Coronation Street, entertained by Emmerdale, barmy about Brookside and nutty about Neighbours. Some storylines were so crazy you would think I'd made them up. So here we go, the top soap moments over the period, drum roll please.

TOP SOAP MOMENTS

EASTENDERS

- WE HAD SONIA AND JAMIE BEING THE KATE WINSLET AND LEONARDO DICAPRIO OF WALFORD.
- EVERY MOMENT WITH IAN BEALE - IS THERE ANYTHING THAT GUY HASN'T BEEN THROUGH?
- DOT COTTON, WHEN SHE GOT ARRESTED FOR CANNABIS POSSESSION BECAUSE SHE THOUGHT IT WAS JUST TEA LEAVES. POSSIBLY MY FAV MOMENT.
- BARRY GETTING MURDERED BY JANINE
- ALL THESE YEARS DIRTY DEN WAS MEANT TO HAVE BEEN KILLED BY ASSASSINATION FOR HIM JUST TURN BACK UP 14 YEARS LATER.. ALIVE.
- KAT SLATER'S "I AM YOUR MOTHER" REVELATION TO ZOE.
- SHARON HAVING A BIT OF BOTH MITCHELL BROTHERS, WITH THAT QUEEN VIC REVEAL. A FEW YEARS LATER SHE WOULD HAVE AN INCESTUOUS RELATIONSHIP WITH DENNIS RICKMAN. OH SHARON. SORT IT OUT GIRL!
- THE MURDER MYSTERY OF THE CENTURY - WHO SHOT PHIL MITCHELL?
- LITTLE MO FIGHTING BACK AGAINST TREVOR WITH THE IRON.

CORONATION STREET

- RAQUEL'S SHOCK DEPARTURE.
- HAYLEY CROPPER TURNING OUT TO BE A TRANS WOMAN.
- TWO WORDS. RICHARD HILLMAN.
- TRACY CRASHING STEVE AND KAREN'S WEDDING.
- BET LYNCH SAYING "ADIOS" TO WEATHERFIELD.

BROOKSIDE

- JIMMY CORKHILL AND THE AMAZING ACTING ABILITY OF DEAN SULLIVAN WHO PLAYED HIM.
- LAD MAG PIN-UP JENNIFER ELLISON PLAYING EMILY SHADWICK.
- BETH AND MARGARET, THE FIRST EVER SAME-SEX KISS TO BE BROADCAST!

EMMERDALE

- THAT MENTAL PLANE CRASH!!
- THAT MENTAL BARN FIRE!!

NEIGHBOURS

- WHEN SUSAN KENNEDY SLIPPED ON MILK AND FORGOT THE LAST 30 YEARS OF HER LIFE.
- HAROLD BISHOP RETURNS FROM THE DEAD.

SONIC THE HEDGEHOG. Video game franchise that started out on the SEGA consoles. Sonic is a little blue hedgehog that runs mental fast, actually he's the fastest thing on the planet. Along with his pals, Tails, Knuckles and Amy he battles to defeat evil.

SONIQUE. Female solo dance artist known mostly for "It Feels So Good" and "Sky". I think she has a vibe of her own, with a lovely crisp voice and it's a shame we didn't hear much more from her.

SOPRANOS, THE. One of the best TV shows ever created with the best leading man in TV drama history. James Gandolfini is perfection as mob boss, Tony Soprano, but all the cast come together to make this show the best around. The scenes with Tony's psychiatrist were amazing and Soprano's last scene was just as memorable as his first scene.

SOUTH PARK. I am talking CLASSIC South Park, episodes from this era only. Cartman was rude, offensive and hilarious, Kenny always got killed. Stan and Kyle were the closest to normal you'd get. Hard to believe they were meant to be only 10 years old. So near the mark at times, it is one of the only TV series that is shock TV but still widely liked. In a time where everything is about political correctness, South Park still manages to get away with poking fun at every race, sex, sexual orientation and anything else you can think of. The creators, Trey Parker and Matt Stone, went on to create "Team America" in 2004, a hilarious satirical comedy using puppets. South Park also had their own movies and a few hit singles too.

SPACED. British sitcom created by Jessica Stevenson and co-created by and starring Simon Pegg. Nick Frost also stars, and Edgar Wright directed, the beginning of the cornetto trio that would later bring you "Shaun of the Dead" etc. The sitcom follows Tim and Daisy, two people that meet by chance and agree to pose as a professional couple to secure a flat. A stoner, geek comedy that doesn't feel dated at all.

SPACE JAM. A movie that is live-action and crossed with animation. Michael Jordan + Looney Tunes = Childhood Classic. Wicked soundtrack thanks to R.Kelly with "I Believe I Can Fly". Perhaps could have been a risky collab but Looney Tunes and Michael Jordan pulled it off!

SPEARS, BRITNEY. I once met a girl who was born in the 90's, who didn't like Britney Spears and I have never cut someone out of my life so fast. Britney fever began with her pop smash, "Hit Me Baby One More Time". We couldn't get enough of her iconic sound. Girls were so excited when she popped up in an episode of "Sabrina the Teenage Witch" and then had Melissa Joan Hart feature in the video for "Crazy". She released a movie, "Crossroads" in 2002 which was not great but…. Britney. This Britney playlist will feel like you are re-living your childhood.

BEST OF BRITNEY

1. BABY ONE MORE TIME - 1998
2. SOMETIMES - 1999
3. CRAZY - 1999
4. BORN TO MAKE YOU HAPPY - 1999
5. OOPS I DID IT AGAIN - 2000
6. LUCKY - 2000
7. STRONGER - 2000
8. DON'T LET ME BE THE LAST TO KNOW - 2001
9. I'M A SLAVE 4 U - 2001
10. OVERPROTECTED - 2001
11. I'M NOT A GIRL, NOT YET A WOMAN - 2002
12. I LOVE ROCK N ROLL - 2002
13. BOYS FT PHARRELL WILLIAMS - 2002
14. ME AGAINST THE MUSIC FT MADONNA - 2003
15. TOXIC - 2004
16. EVERYTIME - 2004

Spice Girls. The band that epitomized the 90's and what all other girl bands aspired to be from then on. Each member had their own look, personality and distinctive voice. You could tell who was singing what, yet when they came together their harmonies were stunning. The band consisted of Mel B/Scary, famed for her wild hair and leopard print. Mel C/Sporty, known for her tracksuits and tomboy vibe. Emma/Baby, the cutesy member with her platinum blonde hair. Geri/Ginger, known for her fiery ginger hair and that incredible union jack dress. Last but not least Victoria/Posh with her perfect brown bob and little black dress. The life changing moment when Geri announced she was leaving and they released "Goodbye" which was too emotional for life with the heart melting lyrics dedicated to her. Their movie "Spiceworld" was watched on repeat by 5 year old me and many other young girls alike.

SPICE UP YOUR PLAYLIST

1. WANNABE - 1996
2. SAY YOU'LL BE THERE - 1996
3. 2 BECOME 1 - 1996
4. MAMA/WHO DO YOU THINK YOU ARE - 1996
5. SPICE UP YOUR LIFE - 1997
6. TOO MUCH - 1997
7. STOP - 1998
8. VIVA FOREVER - 1998
9. GOODBYE - 1998
10. HOLLER - 2000

SPIELBERG, STEPHEN. Legendary director responsible for some of your favourite 90's movies. There were family favourites "Hook" and "Jurassic Park" and the sequel, the incredible and emotional "Schindler's List" and "Saving Private Ryan". Other big movies were "A.I", "Minority Report" and "Catch Me If You Can".

SPIN THE BOTTLE. Popular party game but taken up a notch when the electronic version came out. The buttons would light up for truth, dare or kiss/forfeit. The game was just as effective with a plastic bottle and made up dares, but we still forked out for the electro version anyway.

SPIRIT: STALLION OF THE CIMARRON. Animated movie by Dreamworks and Bryan Adams producing the soundtrack, "Here I Am", was a tune. Spirit is a mustang horse that gets captured by cruel soldiers and their Colonel. A Native-American dude helps rescue him. Spirit then falls in love with one of his female horses and they plan to escape back to the wild. It's infuriating how many times the plan goes tits up. Also, how grim was the opening sequence of that horse pushing out a baby, traumatic!

SPONGEBOB SQUAREPANTS. Again, I'm talking the classic episodes from 1999 and during the early 00's. You know sometimes you can just hear a picture, whenever I see a picture of Spongebob I just hear that infectious little laugh in my head. After all these years, all the serious leaks there's been,

Wikileaks etc and the Krabby Patty formula is still safe. The show even included catchy tunes like the "F.U.N Song", though when you got this stuck in your head every day for a week it did start to grate on you. Whenever there was a bit of carnage there was always that fish that yelled out "Oh my legs!". Such a great cartoon.

SPORTSWEAR. Retro sportswear was huge in the 90's. There were so many brands "Kappa", "Fila", "Champion", "Ellesse", "Puma", "Reebok", of course "Adidas" and "Nike". Popper tracksuit bottoms were super popular in that sort of shiny material. High neck tracksuit jackets were also a much-loved sports item.

SPRINGFIELD, DUSTY (1939-1999). 60's legend Dusty Springfield sadly passed away during this era. Her lovely, delicate voice and 60's style has gone down in British music history. She started her career as part of a trio, "The Springfields" and went onto become a successful solo artist. Her solo career included classics such as "Son of a Preacher Man", "Just Don't Know What to do With Myself" and "Only Want to be With You".

SPY KIDS. Popular children's movie in the 00's about secret agents who fall in love and decide to raise a family of their own. Full of pure cheese.

SPYRO THE DRAGON. One of the most popular platform games ever. The original trilogy was released from 1998-2000. As Spyro the dragon you must release his fellow dragon pals from these crystal jails. Gnasty Gnorc was the main villain in the games and you have this big fight with him at the end.

STANLEY'S MAGIC GARDEN. Also known as "A Troll in Central Park". A lovely children's film with lots of cheese, singing and heart. This movie is unfairly overlooked. It teaches us to not let fear get in the way of our success. It gets a bit Alice in Wonderland-y trippy at times too, which is a visual delight.

STARS IN THEIR EYES. Fun TV show where fans of music artists would transform and do a tribute performance to said artist. The audience would then vote who was the best. By transform I mean literally, they got a makeover to look like their artist of choice and then they performed a song imitating their voice. "Tonight Matthew I am going to be..".

STEFANI, GWEN. A kid asked how to spell bananas recently and it sadly reminded me that we are now living in a post-Gwen world. Firstly, known as the lead singer in the band, "No Doubt", and then went onto find solo success later in the 00's. She loved a space bun and a bindi/face jewels around her eyes. Her solo stuff was a bit too late for this book, but No Doubt's best hits were "Just a Girl", "Spiderwebs", "It's My Life", "Don't Speak" and "Hey Baby".

STEPS. I saw a poster that read "retro 90's night including oldie Steps". OLDIE. RETRO. Someone grab me a chair and some water, I can't deal. British pop group made up of 3 girls and 2 boys. We all thought Faye was well edgy with her blonde dreads.

STEPS BELTERS

1. 5,6,7,8 - 1997
2. LAST THING ON MY MIND - 1998
3. ONE FOR SORROW - 1998
4. HEARTBEAT/TRAGEDY - 1998
5. BETTER BEST FORGOTTEN - 1999
6. LOVE'S GOT A HOLD ON MY HEART - 1999
7. AFTER THE LOVE HAS GONE - 1999
8. SAY YOU'LL BE MINE/BETTER THE DEVIL YOU KNOW - 1999
9. DEEPER SHADE OF BLUE - 2000
10. STOMP - 2000
11. HERE AND NOW/YOU'LL BE SORRY - 2001
12. CHAIN REACTION - 2001

STEREOPHONICS. Fab indie-rock bands ever. The lead singer, Kelly Jones, has the most incredible gritty, powerful voice. Biggest and best hits included "Pick a Part", "Just Looking", "Handbags and the Gladrags" and so many more.

STEWART, JAMES (1908-1997). Beloved actor and military officer. People say Tom Hanks is the modern-day James Stewart, as he was known in the industry to be a kind-hearted and generous man. He starred in, "It's a Wonderful Life" and many other great films including "Philadelphia Story", "Harvey", "Mr Smith Goes to Washington", "Vertigo" and "Rear Window" to name a few! James Stewart was an actor before WW2 but took a break in order to serve his country and rose through the ranks to become a Colonel. It was known he suffered with bad PTSD and was going to quit acting altogether. His portrayal of George Bailey in "It's a Wonderful Life" was hardly acting, more a portrayal of himself. A risk that helped get his acting career back to where it should be. During the 80's he won an honorary academy award but wasn't in the public eye for much longer. He died leaving a lasting influence on American pop culture.

STUART LITTLE. Adorable movie about a talking mouse that gets adopted by the Little family. Great performances by Geena Davis, Hugh Laurie and Jonathan Lipnicki and awesome voice work by Michael J. Fox. Who remembers Stuart's sweet-ass red convertible? If he pulled up next to you at a red light, you'd think …douche. Lead child actor, Jonathan Lipnicki, had other success in this era with his roles in "Jerry Maguire", "Stuart Little 2", "Like Mike", "The Little Vampire" and "Dawson's Creek".

SUGABABES. UK girl group with ever changing members. They seem to be a favourite of director, Richard Curtis, as their songs pop up in his movies a fair bit.

SUGABABES PLAYLIST

1. OVERLOAD - 2000
2. NEW YEAR - 2000
3. RUN FOR COVER - 2001
4. FREAK LIKE ME - 2002
5. ROUND ROUND - 2002
6. STRONGER - 2002
7. ANGELS WITH DIRTY FACES - 2002
8. SHAPE - 2003
9. HOLE IN THE HEAD - 2003
10. TOO LOST IN YOU - 2003
11. IN THE MIDDLE - 2004
12. CAUGHT IN A MOMENT - 2004

SUM 41. Pop-punk band whose main hits were "In Too Deep", "Fat Lip" and "Still Waiting". Even if you were not an avid pop-punk fan you still automatically liked these songs and knew all the lyrics. AND remember them to this day!

SUNNY DELIGHT. Sugary, orange drink that turned your wee bright orange. It also had the potential to turn your skin orange if you drank too much of it (1.5 litres a day according to the news story that came out about the girl that turned orange). One sip and you'll be thrown straight back to childhood.

SUPERMARKET SWEEP. Game show hosted by Dale Winton. What a rush. I used to go to the Tesco Extra store, just to feel something, but this took supermarket fun to new heights. It essentially taught us how to loot as quickly as possible in a crisis. And who didn't want one of those pastel coloured sweatshirts? So 90's chic.

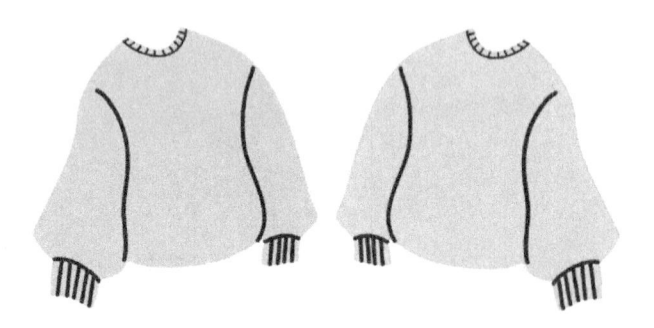

SUPERMODELS. These gorgeous ladies dominated fashion in the 90's. The big six, as they were known, included Naomi Campbell, Christy Turlington, Linda Evangelista, Cindy Crawford, Claudia Schiffer and Kate Moss. Another fashion queen was Tyra Banks, who made history for being the first black woman to appear on her own "Sports Illustrated" cover.

SUPERSOAKER. Wouldn't it be nice if the clocks went back 20 years so I could run around with this huge ass water pistol from NERF. When you got shot you would get SOAKED. Parents didn't dare venture outside in case the kids turned on them.

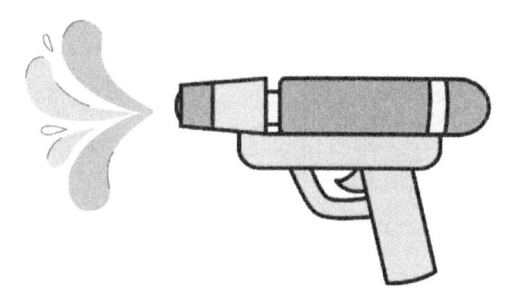

T.

T.A.T.U. Well done us, we've done it again! We've fallen for another music marketing ploy. Remember T.A.T.U's raunchy music video? T.A.T.U were formed up of two ladies and their video for "All the Things She Said" was of them dressed in school uniform snogging each other's faces off! We were gobsmacked at the time, but secretly loved it. Turned out they got outted as fake lesbians just to sell records and they both had male partners. The betrayal!

TAKE THAT. A band whose fan following is probably the biggest out of all UK boy bands. Members of "Take That" included Gary Barlow, Robbie Williams, Mark Owen, Jason Orange and Howard Donald. Total drama when Robbie Williams left and was all cocky, saying he'd be bigger than the band blah blah. Turned out he did become bigger than the band, so fair play.

TAKE THAT TOP TUNES

1. IT ONLY TAKES A MINUTE - 1992
2. A MILLION LOVE SONGS - 1992
3. COULD IT BE MAGIC - 1992
4. PRAY - 1992
5. RELIGHT MY FIRE - 1992
6. BABE - 1993
7. EVERYTHING CHANGES BUT YOU - 1994
8. BACK FOR GOOD - 1995
9. NEVER FORGET - 1995
10. HOW DEEP IS YOUR LOVE - 1996

TALES FROM THE CRYPT. Amazing horror anthology TV show. Short horror stories based on the "Tales From the Crypt" comics, presented by "The Cryptkeeper", a spooky puppet voiced by John Kassir. This show is pun-tastic and so funny. Kids could be scared but it's more comic book horror. The special effects questionable, the gore in your face, a great show.

TAMAGOTCHI. Small electronic virtual pet that gave kids their first taste of parenthood. You couldn't help but worry that your Tamagotchi might get separation anxiety while you were at school. I remember each morning before leaving the house asking my mum to feed my Tamagotchi, and she did. Top grandparenting! You'd try and connect your Tamagotchi with your mates and try and have babies. Easier said than done.

TAMMY GIRL. Popular clothing line for teenage girls. When pocket money just wouldn't stretch to that gorgeous top you saw in "Mizz" and you see some girl from your school wearing it to your friend's party, the sheer hatred and jealousy was real. It's tragic that such an iconic 90's/00's shop is no more.

TAPING THE TOP 40. Every Sunday I would spend several hours sitting by my dad's radio, creating my own mixtapes, pressing the record button every time a banger came on. The annoyance of the DJ talking over the last few seconds of the song! Mixtapes ranged from "Last Resort" by Papa Roach, onto Anastacia "Left Outside Alone", I was oh so eclectic. My mum and dad later confessed they used to crack up with laughter whilst I sat in the backseat of the car, serenading them, unaware of how loud I was singing with my Walkman on. And singing badly I might add, I was no Charlotte Church.

TARANTINO, QUENTIN. Directing royalty who created one of the best scenes in movie history, the dance in the diner with Uma Thurman and John Travolta in "Pulp Fiction". Famous for his graphic use of blood and Asian inspired style, Tarantino brought us many movie favourites in the 90's/early 00's. We had "Reservoir Dogs", "Pulp Fiction", "Jackie Brown" and "Kill Bill: Vol 1". He also wrote "True Romance".

TAZMANIA. Animated TV series about the adventures of popular Looney Tune, Taz. For some reason the 90's loved Taz. Who remembers those Taz chocolate bars that were basically Freddos with caramel?

TAZOS. Round circular discs, similar to Pogs but found in Walkers crisps and were "Looney Tunes" branded. Why don't we get free stuff in crisps now? No clue what you were supposed to do with them, but they were free and people collected them.

TELETUBBIES. Young children's TV show starring Tinky Winky, Dipsy, La-La and Po. No idea if they were a family, a bunch of friends or what. "Tubby Custard and "Tubby Toast" were actual things you could buy. Seeing that pink gooey custard ooze out of the machine was so tempting, it was like the forbidden fruit of childhood. There was a section of the show where a teletubby's stomach square would light up and a video of kids doing some crafting or whatever would play. Then there was the bit where a random object would appear on one of the hills and turn into something. I really remember the lion, a carousel and a house. I don't know how that baby got in the sun but he/she seemed happy so we won't ask too many questions.

TEXAS. Pop-rock band fronted by Sharleen Spiteri. Their first hit "I Don't Wanna Lover" actually came out in 1989 but they had most of their success in the late 90s. Hits like "Inner Smile", "Say What You Want", "Black Eyed Boy" and "Summer Son" were huge in the UK and often made it onto mixtapes.

TFI FRIDAY. TV programme hosted by Chris Evans which signalled the weekend had finally arrived. Chris would interview various celebrities in a bar/party atmosphere. There was always a music guest and random party games. It's your letters!! What a catchy tune. The bar in the studio was actually a real bar and most of the audience were three sheets to the wind.

THELMA AND LOUISE. Classic movie about true friendship, with an all too famous ending. If you and your best bud love perfecting the art of selfies, will protect each other against anything, share the same moral code and will stand by one another no matter what goes down, then you've got your Thelma and Louise relationship down to a tee.

THEME HOSPITAL. What genius thought it would be a grand idea to put us in charge of running a hospital! Super addictive game with funny made up illnesses, like "Bloaty Head", caused by sniffing cheese and cured by popping the head with a pin and re-inflating to normal size. If you haven't played this game, you're 20 years late to the party but it really is still awesome.

THIN BLUE LINE. British sitcom written by Ben Elton and starring Rowan Atkinson. Set in an English police station filled with unique police staff and the many mishaps that occur. Very witty and funny.

THIN EYEBROWS. A trend for women in the 90's/early 00's. Why did we think this was a look? I'm talking about pencil drawn on thin. People really underestimate the power the eyebrow has when it comes to shaping the face and no one looks better with thin eyebrows, ever!

THOMAS THE TANK ENGINE. Every child has at least watched a little bit of Thomas the Tank Engine. The show started in the 80s but carried on through the 90s and 00s. We all think this is a cutesy animation about trains when really it's a show about the fat controller and his evil dictatorship, punishing individuality and rewarding obedience. Kids shows are dark man.

TIMBERLANDS. Our love for hip-hop fashion included the Timberland boot, no link to the rapper and producer of a different spelling. Timberlands are quality workman boots that are waterproof. Apparently, the boots came about due to workman needing something comfortable because they were standing up, on the street during the day and night. Hip-hop fashion wanted to take this hustler look and make it their own. Even more popular than Jordans at one stage would you believe!

TITANIC. The endless debates with friends on how Rose could have saved Jack. We all can clearly see there was room on the door for two, let's move on now. A funny movie in the sense some say it's the worst movie ever made, and some say it's the best. Has anyone rolled in from a drunken night out and flopped on the sofa naked and said, "Paint me like one of your French girls"? No? Just me then. This film won an Oscar in 1997 so to all you haters out there, the academy has spoken. Super romantic and cheesy. "My Heart Will Go On" stirs up emotions we didn't even know we had.

TLC. R&B trio. "No Scrubs" was a tune. I remember never having had a boyfriend before but still being like "HELL YEAH

NO SCRUBZ". Other awesome hits by them were "Unpretty", "Creep" and "Waterfalls".

TOBAR ALIEN EGG. Small gooey alien that was encased in gel and came in its own plastic egg. Used to go furry after one use thanks to carpet fuzz and dust. We were all certain we could make them have babies by placing them back to back or in the fridge.

TOFFO. Sadly, discontinued toffees with different fruity flavours. Reminds me of the sweet taste of being free from braces but probably the reason for all of my fillings now.

TOPLOADER. Band responsible for one of the standout songs of the era "Dancing in the Moonlight". They had a second track which was also good, "Achilles Heel". Sadly, we didn't hear much more after that.

TOTS TV. Tots TV was an underrated children's TV show, using puppets and had a jaunty little theme tune. All the French we learnt was from Tilly. Who didn't want to join the gang? They owned a pet donkey for god's sake!

TOYS IN CEREAL. Why do we not get these breakfast bonuses anymore!? It has totally taken the fun out of breakfast time. My choice of cereal would depend on the quality of the free toy. This needs to make a comeback.

TRACY BEAKER. TV show for young adults based on the book by Jacqueline Wilson about a girl who has been put in a children's home. Tracy was the ultimate sass pot telling everyone to "bog off" all the time. I actually felt really sorry for "Elaine the Pain", everyone hated her, but she was just doing her job. The true hatred was for Justine, what a bi-atch.

TOXIC WASTE. Disgustingly sour sweets that were used as dares or to show how hard you were on the playground. Each colour sweet had a different level of sourness. Even the thought of the black cherry hazardous candy makes my stomach turn and my tongue burn.

TRACY ISLAND. Island from Thunderbirds that Blue Peter taught us how to make in the 90's and you can still get the instructions on the internet today! Kids would do anything back in the day to get a Blue Peter badge and you were a local celeb if you succeeded. I heard that Anthea Turner liked her Tracy Island so much that she actually kept it.

TRAINERS. Sportswear and hip-hop fashion were mega in the 90's. There were several trainers that everyone wanted to wear. There was the "Nike Air Plus" in 1997 and the "Nike Air Max Plus" in 1998. Then the ultimate sought after trainer, 1995's "Nike Air Jordans XI", they sold out every time they were re-

released. In 1996 "Reebok Blast" came out in all their black and white glory. Then there was the "Nike Air Zoom Flight" in 1995 that looked like the kind of shoes you'd fight aliens in. We loved a chunky sole in the 90s. Fila, Sketcher, Vans and DC were great choices for a chunky sole. The "Adidas Supercourt" trainer brought the style of a tennis shoe with a 90's chunkier look.

TRAINSPOTTING. Very dark, very adult movie about drug abuse. Directed by Danny Boyle and starring Ewan McGregor as lead character Renton, a young man wrapped up in the Edinburgh drug scene. The movie is so good but there are some super upsetting scenes so if you haven't seen it be warned.

TYCOON GAMES. Various games under the "Tycoon" family, all following the same format of creating your own and then running it. Stand out titles were "Rollercoaster Tycoon", "Zoo

Tycoon" and "Mall Tycoon" but there are so many more. Another game like "Rollercoaster Tycoon" is "Theme Park". Once again, we were given responsibility and the power went to our heads. The most messed up things we did on "Rollercoaster Tycoon" was drop an unhappy guest in the lake or force guests to ride an unfinished rollercoaster to their deaths. What is wrong with us!?

TV ADVERTS. There's been some iconic TV ads during this period that are unforgettable. See how many of these ring a bell.

90'S & 00'S CLASSIC ADS

1. ROLOS - THE CINEMA ONE AND THE SKIPPY ONE
2. TANGO - ALL OF THEM FROM 91-97
3. LEVI'S - FLAT ERIC
4. BUDWEISER - THE FROGS AND WAZZZZZUP
5. JOHN SMITH - ALL THE PETER KAY ADVERTS
6. CHEWITS - I LIKE TO CHEWIT CHEWIT
7. WALLS - THE ANGRY DOG
8. THE SHEILAS - SHEILAS WHEELS
9. JAFFA CAKES - TOTAL ECLIPSE!
10. CRUNCHIE - CHOCOLATE ROLLERCOASTER
11. REEBOK - THE BELLY
12. DAIM - ARMADILLO
13. MCCAIN CHIPS - CHIPS OR DADDY?
14. BN BISCUITS - BN BN DOO DOO DA DOO DOO
15. TOYS R US - TOYS OF A MILLION ALL UNDER ONE ROOF
16. IRN BRU CHRISTMAS ADVERT - THE SNOWMAN PARODY
17. JOHN WEST - BEAR FIGHT
18. BARCLAYS - SAMUEL L JACKSON
19. HALIFAX - HOWARD

TV ON WHEELS. The excitement when you were in class and you could hear the wheels of the TV rolling your way. It would always be a well boring science video, but hey a video is better than an actual lesson, right!?

TWAIN, SHANIA. Country-pop singer who gave us the most badass female empowerment song of the 90's, "Man I Feel Like A Woman" and that sexy leopard print jumpsuit in the video for "That Don't Impress Me Much". Other big hits were "You're Still the One" and "From This Moment On".

TWEENIES. Children's TV show starring Bella, Fizz, Milo and Jake. They even had a few hit singles and an album! Their biggest singles were "Best Friends Forever" and "Number 1". How influential was that spinning "Tweenie Clock"? Imagine if you spun a wheel every morning and it decided what you were going to do that day. Oh, so spontaneous!

TWIN PEAKS. An amazing TV series we have David Lynch to thank for! A surreal and unique murder mystery, posing the famous question, who killed Laura Palmer? Each character adds something to the show and it's so stylish. "Diane, the cherry pie and black coffee is damn fine here in Twin Peaks".

TWO PINTS OF LAGER AND A PACKET OF CRISPS. British sitcom about 5 friends and their lives together. Some are coupled up and some are unlucky in love. The series often end on a cliff-hanger on whether various couples will stay together or not.

TYSON, MIKE. Dominated heavyweight boxing in the 90's with help from his crazy reputation. In the mid to late 80's Tyson came firing onto the scene, known for his ridiculous speed, intimidating other boxers because he would just come at them. His opponents focused so hard on getting the dodge in because when that punch came flying at you it was goodnight Vienna. His career wasn't going as well for him in the 90's. He fought Holyfield in 1996, lost, had a re-match and knowing he would lose again resorted to that famous ear bite which got him disqualified.

U.

U2. One of the biggest bands on the planet continued their long line of successful hits well into the 90's and 00's. Teaming up with Boyzone for "The Sweetest Thing" and giving us hits such as, "One", "Beautiful Day" and "Elevation".

UM BONGO. Tropical juice with animals on the carton. The carton was much sturdier than other juices, such as Capri Sun. Who remembers pushing their straw through the hole of a Capri Sun and it going all the way through? Why do bad things happen to good people?

USHER. Very popular R&B artist in the 90's/early 00's. Major floorfiller "Yeah" had us all on the dancefloor and perfecting our Lil John impressions. Other big hits included "You Make Me Wanna", "Pop Ya Collar", "U Remind Me", "U Got It Bad" and the "Singstar" favourite, "Burn".

US TEEN SOAPS. Our love for soaps stretched across the globe. Big titles including "One Tree Hill", "90210", "Dawson's Creek" and "The OC". They always had killer theme tunes, The OC with Phantom Planet's "California", One Tree Hill with Gavin Degraw's "I Don't Wanna Be". The OC featured a man with the most magnificent eyebrows ever seen.

V.

VANILLA ICE. Ice Baby! Contrary to his name, Vanilla Ice was hot stuff. An American rapper who ripped off David Bowie/Queen's "Under Pressure" to give us "Ice Ice Baby".

VELVET. Popular material for clothes to be made out of in the 90's. Pink velvet t-shirts, black velvet blazers, green velvet dresses. Stunning and glorious to touch.

VELVET ART. A piece of artwork made from velvet, designed for you to colour in and display. Often of a movie or TV character. You would give them to your parents as gifts, but they never made it into a photo frame, so you'd just have random piles of them in your home.

VENGABOYS, THE. Euro-dance/pop group famous for such classics as "Ibiza", "Boom Boom Boom Boom" and "Venga Party".

VERSACE, GIANNI (1946-1997). Italian fashion designer who was tragically assassinated outside his home in Miami, Florida. He was an unbelievable designer and visionary, kitting out famous people such as Princess Diana, Madonna and other celebrities. He was famous for bold prints, most famously the head of Medusa, which would pop up in his designs. His sister, Donatella Versace, carried on the brand after his tragic passing and is still a huge success today, moving into accessories and home furnishings as well.

VHS OPENINGS. Who can forget the sound of the BBC videos in the 90's or the Disney castle and music before each film? Just the sound makes my heart hurt.

VICAR OF DIBLEY. Very funny sitcom starring Dawn French as Geraldine Granger, a female vicar. One of the best British sitcoms ever starring some of the nation's biggest talents. From the moment Geraldine first arrived in Dibley when everyone was blatantly expecting a bloke. To when she was getting to know the village's unique residents and telling terrible jokes to Alice, there isn't an episode that doesn't leave you with a smile on your face.

VIRAL VIDEOS. How much did we wee ourselves when we watched those videos that made you look closer into the screen to see if you can spot something and then out of nowhere a horrific screaming demon comes blaring out your speakers. NOT COOL MAN. There were lots of videos that went viral in the late

90's/early 00's and considering there was no YouTube until 2005, this was pretty impressive.

FORGOTTEN VIRAL VIDS

1. THE FLEA MARKET
2. SHOES
3. THE EMO SONG
4. LONDON UNDERGROUND
5. DRAMATIC CHIPMUNK
6. CHOCOLATE RAIN
7. LEEROY JENKINS
8. NUMA NUMA MAN
9. CHARLIE THE UNICORN
10. PEANUT BUTTER JELLY
11. DANCING BABY
12. EVOLUTION OF DANCE
13. CHARLIE BIT ME
14. MAGICAL TREVOR
15. ULTIMATE SHOWDOWN OF ULTIMATE DESTINY
16. LLAMA SONG
17. BADGER BADGER
18. SALAD FINGERS
19. KID TERRIFIED BY THE SCARY MAZE

VIRGIN MEGASTORE. This shop was THE place to go to get albums, DVDs, games, merch and books. Killed by online streaming.

W.

WALKING WITH BEASTS. Fascinating one-off show that showed us the world at the time of woolly mammoths and sabre-toothed tigers. The animation was state of the art at the time, we were mind blown by the recreation of all the animals and beasts of the past.

WALKMAN. Kids of today will never know the struggle of trying to fit your Walkman in your jeans or jacket pocket. Also when you went over a bump in the road and it skipped the song, just as it was getting to the chorus and you were about to get down.

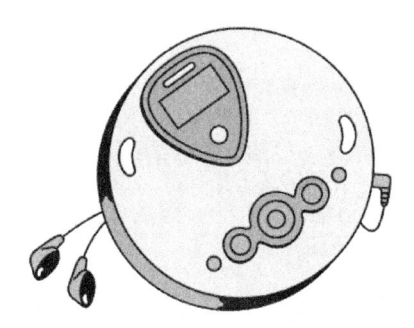

WALLACE AND GROMIT. Clay animated characters created by Nick Park. We need one of those beds in our lives, how speedy would it be to get ready in the morning! The duo started off in their own TV series and progressed into movies like "The Wrong Trousers" and "A Close Shave".

WAYNE'S WORLD. This, alongside Austin Powers, are Mike Myers best films. Wayne and Garth are two goofball Queen fans who have their own small time TV show and can't believe their luck when a TV network wants to hire them. The characters actually began on American favourite, "SNL". Another fun fact, the movie itself was shot in just 34 days!

WEAKEST LINK, THE. Quiz show hosted by the ice queen herself, Anne Robinson. Anne also provided us with gameshow's most famous line "You are the weakest link, goodbye".

WESTLIFE. Ireland's top boy band along with Boyzone. Members included Shane Filan, Bryan McFadden, Markus Feehily, Kian Egan and Nicky Byrne. This band had the "getting up off the stool" move down to a tee.

THE WESTLIFE PLAYLIST

1. SWEAR IT AGAIN - 1999
2. IF I LET YOU GO - 1999
3. FLYING WITHOUT WINGS - 1999
4. I HAVE A DREAM - 1999
5. SEASONS IN THE SUN - 1999
6. FOOL AGAIN - 2000
7. MY LOVE - 2000
8. WHAT MAKES A MAN - 2000
9. UPTOWN GIRL - 2001
10. WHEN YOU'RE LOOKING LIKE THAT - 2001
11. QUEEN OF MY HEART - 2001
12. BOP BOP BABY - 2002
13. WORLD OF OUR OWN - 2002
14. UNBREAKABLE - 2002
15. TONIGHT - 2003

WHAT NOT TO WEAR. Before Gok, there were Trinny and Susannah, telling us what and what not to wear for our body shape. Subtlety was not their forte, "Disgusting, big breasted women should NEVER wear horizontal stripes, what were you thinking!" I guess they meant well but they were totally savage. Trinny and Susannah told ladies to get a bra that fits properly and HOIK them up (not sure if they invented that word but they couldn't get enough of saying it). And always accentuate the waist.

WHERE ARE THEY? BOOKS. Great seek and find books, similar to "Where's Wally". It was a small victory when you managed to find the main characters quickly. Titles included "Search for Sam" and "Find Freddie".

WHO WANTS TO BE A MILLIONAIRE? Quiz show that has seen resurgence in recent years but I'm talking about the Chris Tarrant years. SPECIFICALLY 2001, when Charles Ingram caused the biggest game show controversy, cheating his way to the million pound prize with the help of his wife and friend. He had someone coughing in the audience, directing him to the right answers. When we watched it live we were all so oblivious, but then you watch it back and you're like "How did we not know!?". Tarrant himself said he was totally fooled at the time and didn't notice anything suspect, crazy.

WILD THORNBERRYS, THE. Animated show on Nickelodeon. We wished our family were as cool as the Thornberrys. Eliza was an inspirational character for young girls but Debbie was the coolest girl out there. She was the epitome of teen angst, so grunge and never changed who she was. The Wild Thornberrys had their own movie in 2002 and then they did a crossover in 2003 with the "Rugrats"! What a collab.

WILL AND GRACE. US sitcom that made TV history for having the first openly gay character in a lead role. Will is a lawyer working his way up, his old high school girlfriend is Grace. Will took a while to come out to Grace but had the help of his bestie, Jack (also gay). Will and Grace remained best friends and they shared an apartment together. The show is about them two, Jack and his bestie Karen. The show isn't about romantic love, but unconditional love and unbreakable friendships.

WILLIAMS, ROBBIE. One of the bestselling artists of all time. Starting his career off in "Take That", Robbie left the band, and his solo career took off. He tried to break America but they were having none of it, still the UK were mad for him.

THE ROBBIE WILLIAMS ONE

1. FREEDOM - 1996
2. OLD BEFORE I DIE - 1997
3. ANGELS - 1997
4. LET ME ENTERTAIN YOU - 1998
5. MILLENIUM - 1998
6. NO REGRETS - 1998
7. STRONG - 1999
8. SHE'S THE ONE - 1999
9. ROCK DJ - 2000
10. KIDS FT KYLIE MINOGUE - 2000
11. SUPREME - 2000
12. ETERNITY - 2001
13. SOMETHIN STUPID FT NICOLE KIDMAN - 2001
14. FEEL - 2002
15. COME UNDONE - 2003

WILLIAMS, ROBIN. Hilarious comedian and actor, known as the man of 1000 voices. A man with the unique ability to provide laughs for all ages. Some of his most loved movies were box office flops would you believe! His best movies over this period include "Hook", "Aladdin", "Mrs Doubtfire", "Jumanji", "Good Will Hunting" and the very sinister "One Hour Photo".

WILLIAMS SISTERS, THE. Gosh, those Williams sisters when they play tennis don't half make a racquet! Venus and Serena Williams are the youngest of 5 sisters and were taught the art of tennis by their father from a very young age. Venus won her first Wimbledon in 2000, the sisters stayed up until 2am partying and then casually won the doubles the next day. What of it. By 2002 Serena's game improved and she won Wimbledon and knocked Venus off the top spot as tennis female No.1. Competitiveness on the court has made the sisters closer rather than pulling them apart.

WILSON, JACQUELINE. The 90's saw the rise of much-loved children's author Jacqueline Wilson and her illustrator Nick Sharratt. Together they created magical and relatable stories for children and young adults. Some even got turned into TV shows and TV movies. The "Tracy Beaker" TV series was massive, along with "Girls in Love".

WINDBREAKERS. Those waterproof jackets with patches of colour on them were so big in the 80's and 90's. Everyone's mum had a turquoise one with a bit of pink or purple in it.

WIZADORA. Children's TV show about a trainee witch, her bizarre friends and their adventures. I do wonder if the creators of some children's TV are trippin' when designing the characters. Stan the Shopkeeper was played by comedy legend, Brian Murphy, from "George and Mildred". Great kids show.

WOODS, TIGER. How much do we love it when a "thug life" bird lands on the golf course? That's how exciting golf gets. However, another animal made us beam from ear to ear during the early 00's and that was Tiger Woods. Tiger first turned pro in 1996 and was the youngest person to complete a career GrandSlam in 2000. He was also the youngest Masters champion ever at a mere 21 years old.

WOOLWORTHS. Going shopping with your mum or dad was boring but there was one shop that made it all worthwhile. After your parent had gotten over the rage of being catfished by a parking spot they thought was free, only to find a KA in it. They forced you to walk around shop after shop for what felt like an eternity. Then at the end, you would start walking towards the red glow of the Woolworths sign and life was good again. No exaggeration here, the saddest loss to the British High Street and the UK as a whole. THE PICK A MIX, why didn't someone save it!? Whenever I see a Woolworths tote bag, I tear up a bit.

WORMS. Video game that came out in 1995 with a sequel, "Worms Armageddon" in 1997. It was a tactical game where you had to fire weapons and go to the war with the opposite team of worms. As with everything we would name the members of our team after family and friends and get way too invested in waging war. "Incoming!", "Kamikaze".

WORST WITCH, THE. Book series by Jill Murphy which later turned into a great BBC TV series. All girls wanted to be Mildred Hubble in Miss Cackle's Academy.

WOTSITS OVEN CHIPS. A cheesy, potatoy, taste sensation. They were 100% real though no one seems to remember them. Super yummy and needs to come back so I can prove their existence.

WWE. In the 90's you would have known pro wrestling as the World Wrestling Federation A.K.A WWF. However, in the early 00's, World Wildlife Fund weren't having any of it and they had to change their name to World Wrestling Entertainment, known as WWE. In the late 90's were you one of the millions of fans who smelt what the Rock was cooking? Maybe you knew your role, shut your mouth and just sat back and embraced everything the WWE had to offer. Long before this period of wrestling there were the greats of yesteryear including the likes of Hulk Hogan, Macho Man Randy Savage and Jake the Snake Roberts, when it was all about being a true American hero. Then at the 1996 "King of the Ring", everything changed as the victor of this prized and valued tournament took to the mic. You might know him as the Texas Rattlesnake. Stone Cold Steve Austi had just beaten the legend Jake Roberts in the final. He turned directly to the camera and said "You talk about your John 3:16, well Austin 3:16 says I just whipped your ass". This sparked the start of the Attitude Era in wrestling and by heck it was certainly full of attitude. From Austin to the Rock, Triple H to the Undertaker, this form of entertainment was like nothing you'd seen before and nothing you'll see again. Only in the late 90's and early 00's could you go from seeing Mick Foley's persona of Mankind being thrown off a 20ft structure through an announcers table to Mae Young, a woman in her 80s giving birth to a hand. Mental, yet WWE got away with it and we loved them for it.

TOP WRESTLERS OF THE ATTITUDE ERA

1. THE ROCK
2. STONE COLD
3. TRIPLE H
4. KANE
5. CHRIS JERICHO
6. THE UNDERTAKER
7. KURT ANGLE
8. MICK FOLEY
9. THE DUDLEY BOYS
10. THE BIG SHOW
11. TRISH STRATUS
12. SHANE MCMAHON
13. SHAWN MICHAELS
14. X-PAC
15. ROAD DOGG
16. BILLY GUNN
17. CHYNA
18. RIKISHI
19. EDGE
20. CHRISTIAN
21. THE HARDY BOYS
22. LITA

X.

XBOX. The first Xbox was released in 2002 by Microsoft, designed to rival the PS2. With Nintendo and PS2 at large everyone thought Xbox would be a bit of a flop. But how wrong we were! Best original games at the time were "Halo 2", "Elder Scrolls 3" and "Fable".

XENA WARRIOR PRINCESS. TV show that got all the fantasy nerds a bit hot under the collar. Xena and her sidekick Gabrielle had a beautiful relationship, there was always a "more than friend vibe" but they never got together. Ares, the God of War, always had a bit of a hold on Xena, she secretly loved him and thus Gabrielle and Xena never were. Xena travelled around kicking ass and fighting evil with Gabrielle, who ensured she stayed on the straight and narrow.

X FILES, THE. Sci-Fi, detective show with a famous theme tune. Mulder and Scully, one of the most iconic TV duos ever. A real cult classic that had us hooked, determined to join the search for the truth. Playing on our deepest fears of conspiracy theories, mythology and monsters, the show is as relevant today as it was back then.

Y.

Y2K BUG. Spoiler alert, the Y2K bug never happened. Also known as the Millennium Bug, the Y2K bug was a problem in the coding of all technology. It was apparently going to wreak havoc on all computer systems and electronics around the world. So many experts had warned us the computers won't be able to cope with everything changing to 1/1/2000, huge sums were prepped, we were warned planes would fall from the sky and power stations would melt. No idea what all the fuss was about because this did not happen. I believe the computer programmers out there worked their butts off preventing this from happening and it's thanks to them we survived Y2K.

Z.

ZZZAP! Quirky children's TV show that makes you wish we still lived in the weirdness that was the 90's. Set out like a comic book and each frame had a different character. There was "Daisy Dares You", "Smarty Arty", "The Handymen" and "Cuthbert Lilly". It was proper old-fashioned entertainment, with lots of magic and slapstick comedy.

ZOMBIE, ROB. Heavy rock artist who gave us headbangers, "Dragula" and "Living Dead Girl". Rob is also an amazing director, in 2003 he released the first of his horror trilogy "House of 1000 Corpses" with the famous Captain Spaulding. All his films are so good and so visually exciting, if a little gory to say the least.

0-10

2PAC (1971-1996). Tupac Shakur, A.K.A 2Pac, is one of the biggest rappers of all time, a true urban poet. His death at such a young age was so unfortunate, sadly he was linked with gang warfare and was shot by a rival gang. Known by his rabbit ear style bandana and nose piercing, 2Pac was iconic in look and sound. Best hits were "Dear Mama", "California Love ft Dr Dre", "Changes" and "Thugz Mansion".

2 UNLIMITED. Eurodance group who had lots of success in the UK with "Get Ready For This", "Twilight Zone", "Workaholic", "No Limits" and "Tribal Dance".

2POINT4 CHILDREN. An underrated BBC sitcom. The show followed the Porter family and all their unfortunate mishaps. The title was created by taking the average number of children per household in the UK, the .4 because the dad was still very basically a child too. A cult classic because of its dark and surreal moments.

24. Popular US drama about Jack Bauer, an agent working for the counter terrorist department, working to stop various attacks happening on innocent people. Each episode was real-time, a different day, a different terrorist attack to prevent. It was one of a kind.

3 FRIENDS AND JERRY. Animated Nickelodeon show that no one seems to remember. It followed the adventures of four 10-year-old boys, lusting over but pretending not to lust over a group of girls from their school. They always used to get into crazy situations, sort of like a kid friendly "South Park".

5IVE. UK boy band made up of five members, Jay, Abz, Ritchie, Scott and Sean. Abz was a great poster boy for those that liked the sort of chav hot. Best songs were "Keep on Movin", "Got the Feelin", "When the Lights Go Out", "If Ya Gettin Down", "Slam Dunk Da Funk", "Everybody Get Up" and "Let's Dance".

8 SIMPLE RULES. For dating my teenage daughter. US sitcom about a family with three children, two daughters and a son. The oldest is just hitting the dating scene, the other daughter is lacking in self-confidence and the son is just getting into girls. The show is a funny take on what it's like raising teenagers and the funny situations they get themselves into.

10 THINGS I HATE ABOUT YOU. The English teacher in this has got to be one of the most underappreciated movie characters. Every line he has is comedy gold and he deserved more screen

time. This movie was a modern adaptation of Shakespeare's "Taming of the Shrew".

11 O'CLOCK SHOW, THE. Satirical, British comedy featuring on-trend sketches and commentary on the news. Ali G first featured on this show, Ricky Gervais also found fame on it too. Charlie Brooker was one of the writers on the show along with Roger Drew.

50 CENT. 2003 saw 50 Cent find some mainstream fame with big hits "In Da Club", "21 Questions" and "PIMP". He was the villain everyone loved, apart from Ja Rule, Ja Rule was not a fan. 50's album "Get Rich or Die Tryin" was a huge success, we've always had a soft spot for a bad guy.

911. Three-piece boy band who had success with hits "Little Bit More", "Private Number" and "More Than A Woman".

-Closing Time-

About The Author

Daisy Watson is an author, nostalgist and pop culture enthusiast. Her idols are sadly dead or made up. These include Bogie and Bacall, Johnny Cash, Alexander McQueen and Peggy Bundy from "Married with Children". Daisy enjoys fashion, her eclectic music taste, conspiracies and the quirky side of life. She wants to be Dita Von Teese when she grows up. The A-Z of Nostalgia 90's and Early 00's Edition is her first book.

www.daisywatson.com